EL ANATSUI A Sculpted History of Africa

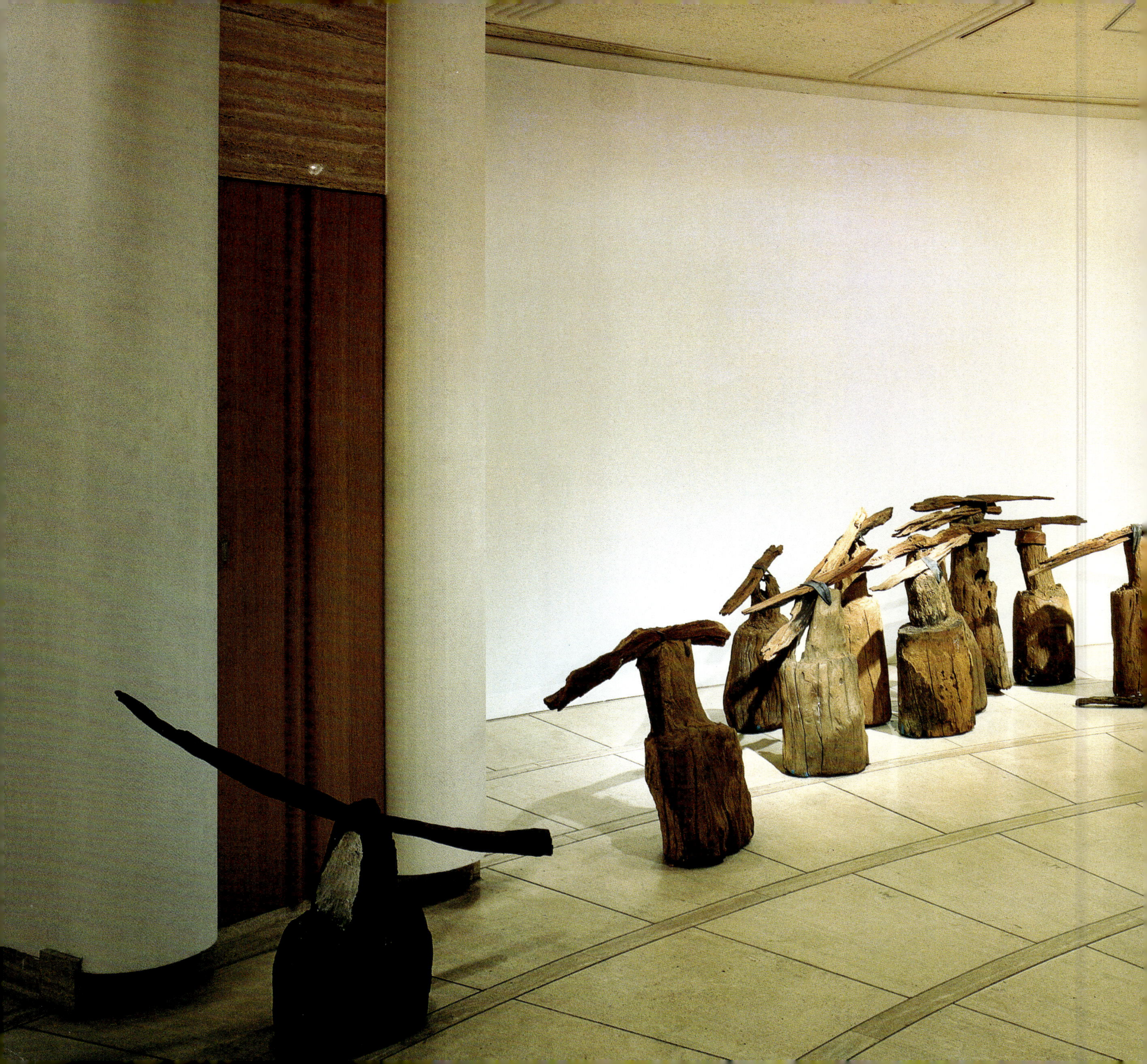

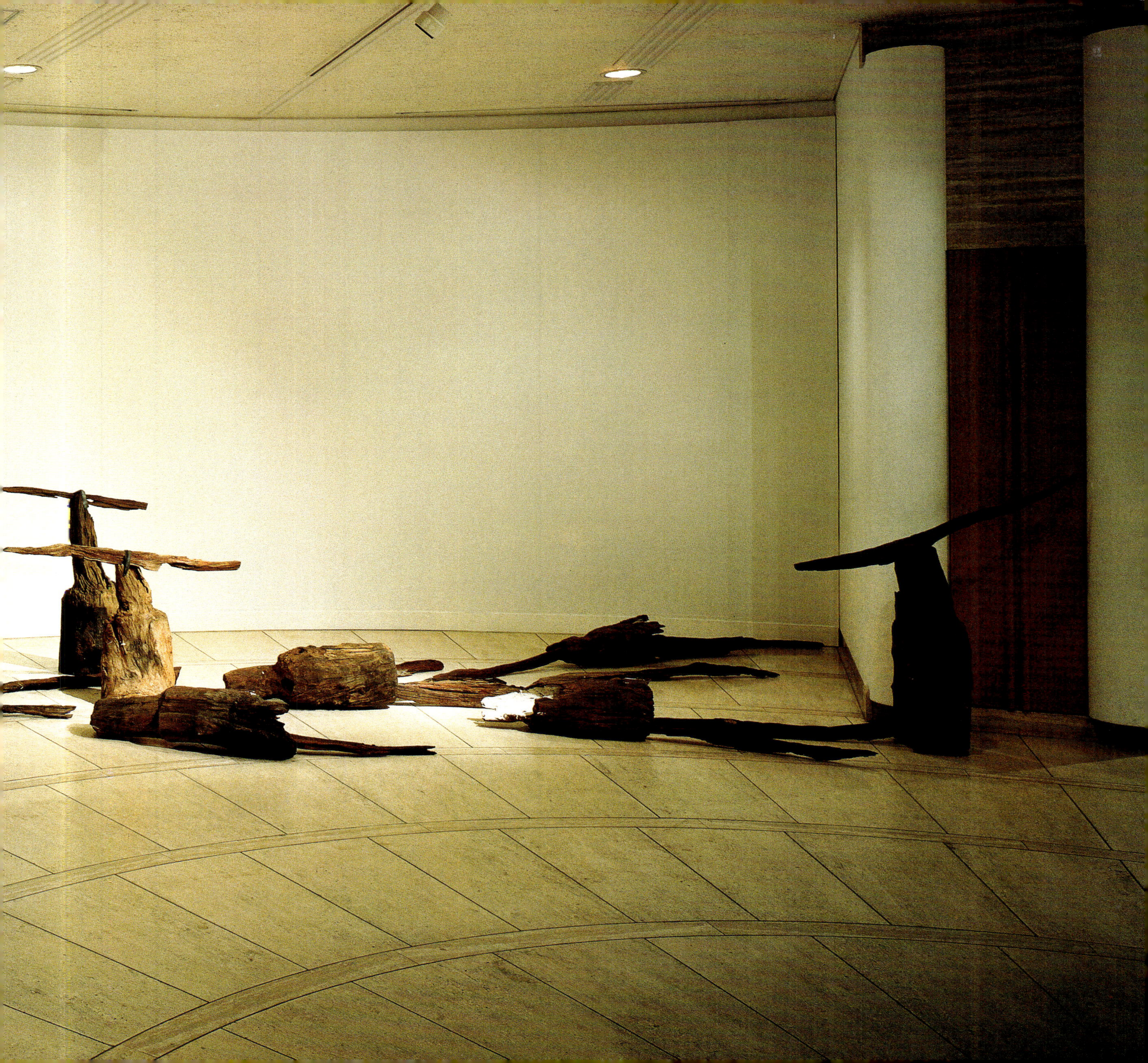

OVERLEAF

On Their Fateful Journey Nowhere, 1995

installation, okpeye wood
height 92cm, width & depth variable
Collection of the Setagaya Art Museum, Tokyo

Photo: Norihiro Ueno

EL ANATSUI

A Sculpted History of Africa

John Picton *with*
Gerard Houghton
Yukiya Kawaguchi
Elisabeth Lalouschek
Simon Njami
Elizabeth Péri-Willis

Funded by THE ARTS COUNCIL OF ENGLAND

Published by Saffron Books in conjunction with the October Gallery, London

Saffron BOOKS

African Art and Society Series
Series Editor Sajid Rizvi

El Anatsui: A Sculpted History of Africa

John Picton *with* Gerard Houghton, Yukiya Kawaguchi, Elisabeth Lalouschek, Simon Njami and Elizabeth Péri-Willis

Cover: *Unfolding the Scroll of History II, 1994* (detail)

ISBN 1-872843-14-X

Published by Saffron Books, an imprint of Eastern Art Publishing

P O Box 13666
London SW14 8WF
United Kingdom

Telephone +44-[0]-181-392 1122
Facsimile +44-[0]-181-392 1422
E-Mail EasternArt@compuserve.com

In conjunction with
The October Gallery
24 Old Gloucester Street
London WC1N 3AL
United Kingdom

Telephone +44-[0]-171-242 7367
Facsimile +44-[0]-171-405 1851
E-Mail OctoberGallery@compuserve.com

Printed by Amica Fine Art Print, London
Telephone +44-[0]-181-670 6060

British Library Cataloguing in Publication Data

A catalogue record of this book is available from the British Library

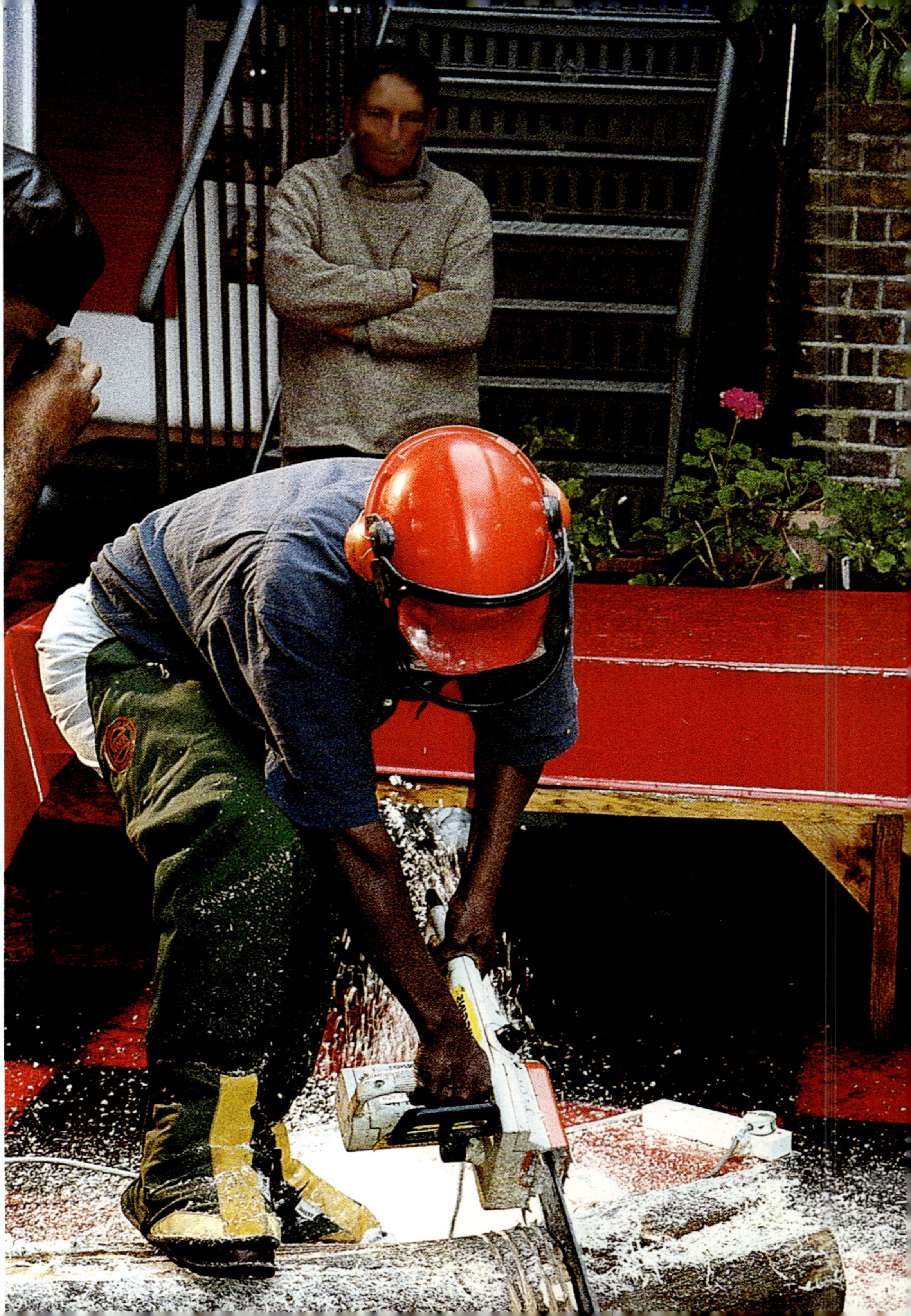

Contents

Acknowledgments **11**

Foreword **13**

John Picton
'Patches of history' patching up my art history: some reflexions on the sculpture of El Anatsui, 1998 **17**

Gerard Houghton
El Anatsui and the Transvangarde **27**

Catalogue Plates **37-55**

Yukiya Kawaguchi (Japanese and English Texts)
A Fateful Journey **56**

Elisabeth Lalouschek
Ein Künstler der Transvangarde: Weltansichten und Weltgeschichten **65**

Simon Njami
Un artiste sur le fil de l'histoire **71**

Elizabeth Péri-Willis
Chambers of Memory **79**

Milestones **89**

Bibliography **93**

Index **95**

Opposite Page

El Anatsui working on found wood at the October Gallery, 1995

Photo: Craig Inglis

I look at the textures of my work in progress
And I think about the texture and grain of Africa's History.

I look at the authentic colours of the different types of wood
And they remind me of the real colours of Africa's History.

I contemplate the directions of the large populations of mobile figures
And they replicate the migrations in Africa's History.

I look at the variegated circumstances on the face of a large figure just created
And the feeling takes me across the face of Africa's History.

— El Anatsui

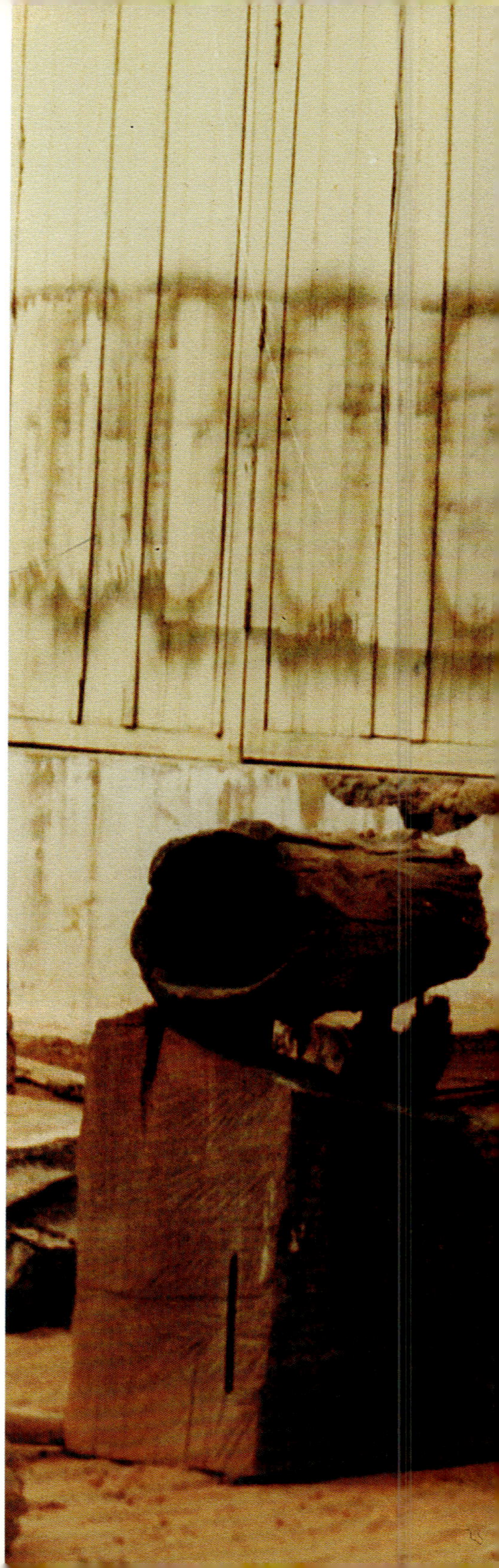

El Anatsui at his studio in Nsukka, 1997

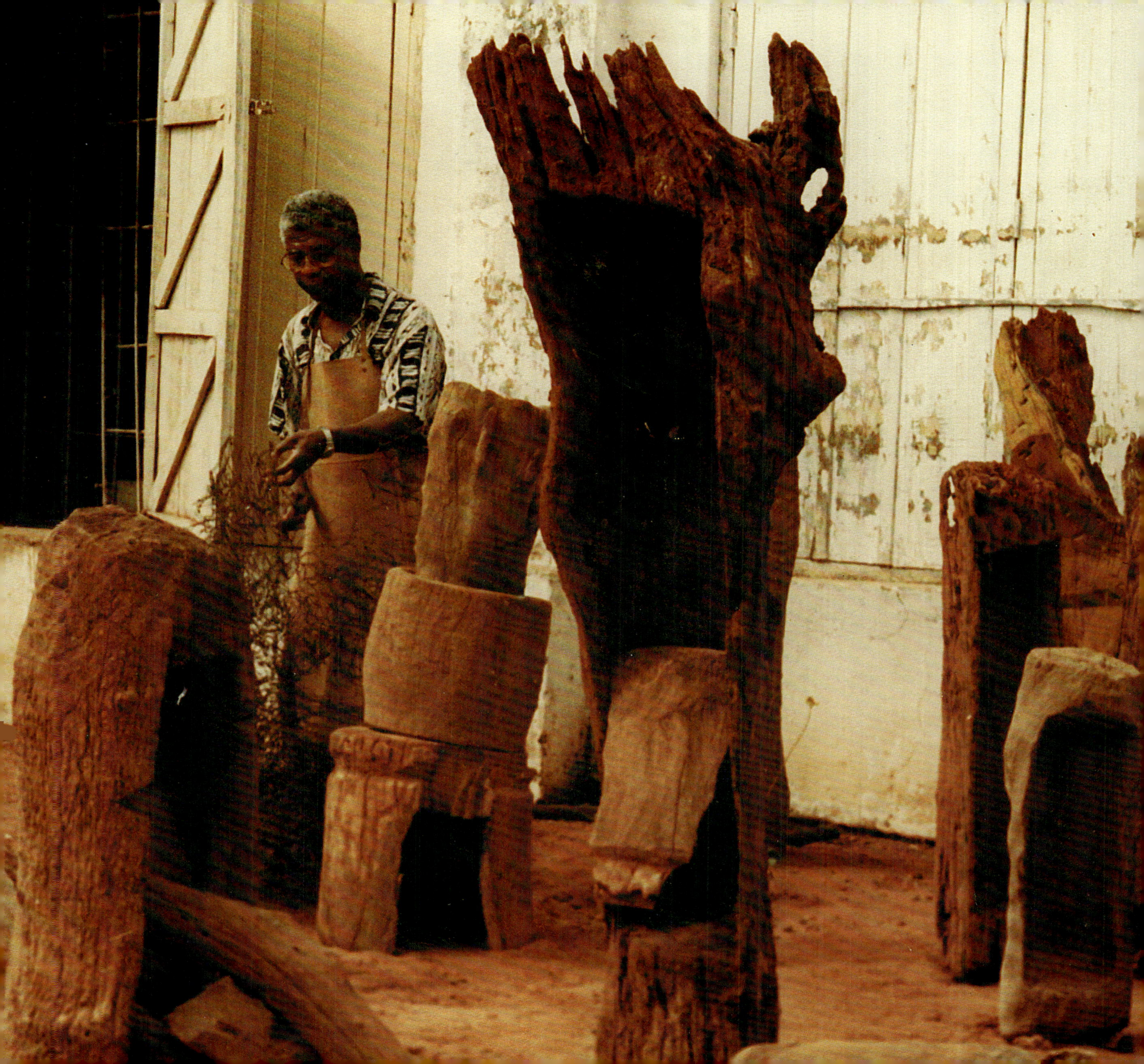

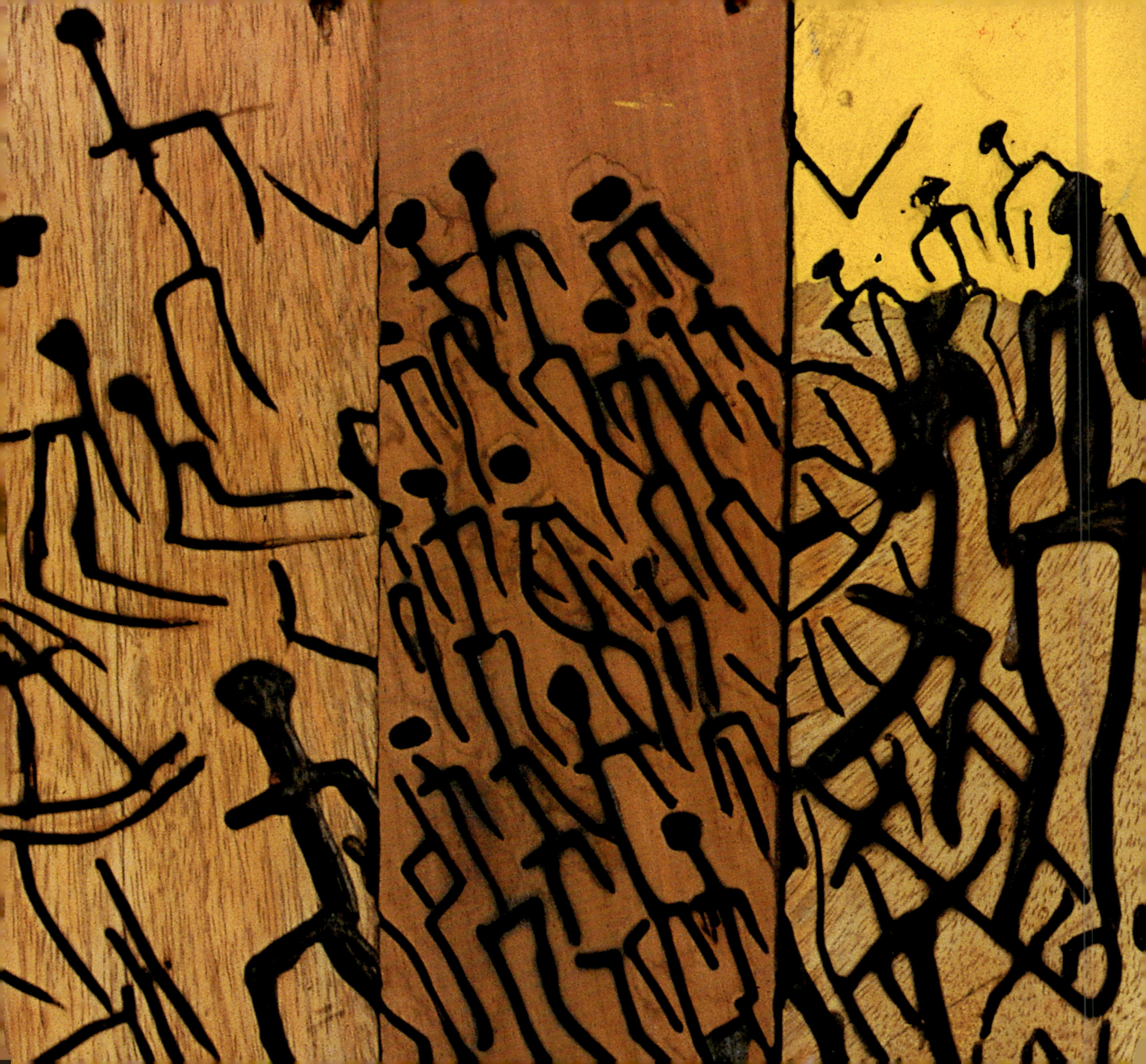

Acknowledgments

This volume, a sequel to *Art Criticism and Africa** in the African Art and Society Series, is the result of a collaboration between ourselves and the October Gallery, London, which makes it doubly unusual. Other planned titles in the series are focused on the wider picture, the artistic developments and trends that are seen to impact on communities or groups on the continent and in diaspora. A whole book devoted to an individual artist has been included in the series because, in our view, El Anatsui represents a significant body of work, not only his own creations but also those of his predecessors and contemporaries, as well as numerous African artists who are known to be out there but are yet to enter the limelight. This explains and in turn is explained by the title, *El Anatsui: A Sculpted History of Africa.*

The book is also unusual because of its multilingual content. Some specialists may look askance at multilingual texts, believing that such ventures dilute the scholarly vigour of a publication. This scepticism borders on arrogant presumption. A multilingual volume opens new vistas and reveals to those not yet initiated the surprising accessibility and power of an artist's oeuvre. Many people have been humbled, for example, by the Japanese interest in African art.

While seconding acknowledgments that follow from Chili Hawes, I am especially grateful to Gerard Houghton for his supervision of the commissioning and editing of the English, French and Japanese texts and to Elisabeth Lalouschek not only for her German-language essay but for collaboration throughout the various stages of production. My debt to *Eastern Art Report* co-editor Shirley Rizvi mounts, for having put up, once again, with demanding schedules and cast her vigilant eye over the whole project, from the planning and editing processes to the last detail of design before going to press.

Sajid Rizvi
Series Editor, African Art and Society

*Deepwell, K (ed), *Art Criticism and Africa* [London: Saffron Books, 1997, ISBN 1-872843-13-1] resulted from a 1996 conference organised at the Courtauld Institute in London by the International Association of Art Critics (AICA). It includes essays by Fatma Ismail Afifi, David Koloane, Murray McCartney, Tony Mhonda, Barbara Murray, Everlyn Nicedemus, Olu Oguibe, Chika Okeke, Ola Oloidi, John Picton, Colin Richards, George Shire and Olabisi Silva.

Unfolding the Scroll of History II, 1994 (detail)

wood relief, oke-ofo, oyili-oji, akparata, okpo-ocha woods & tempera
height 61cm, 141 cm, depth 2.5cm

Photo: Andy Keate

Colour plate on p40

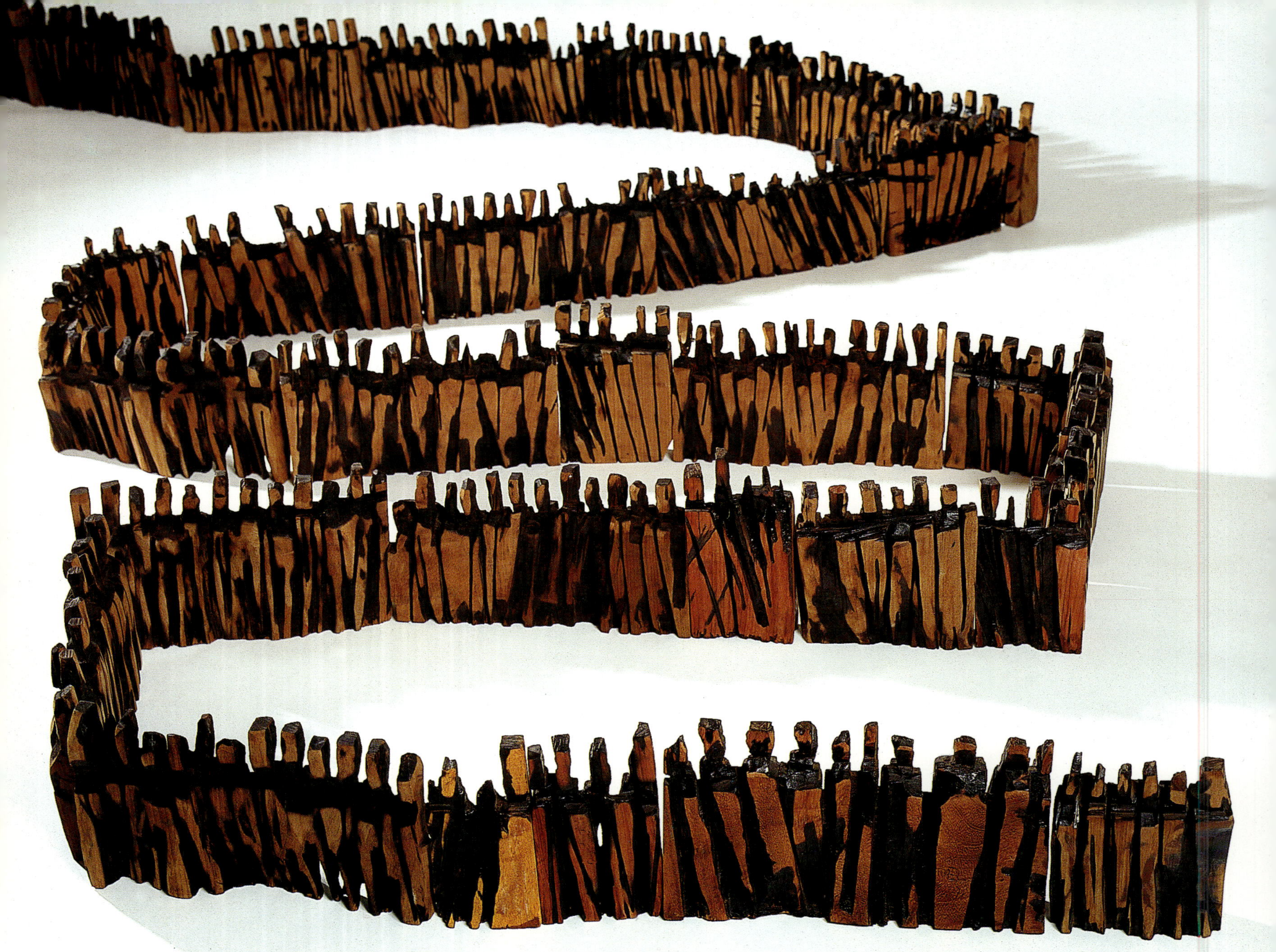

Visa Queue, 1992

installation, oyili-oji, opepe & camwood
height 20cm, width & depth variable

Photo: Andy Keate

Foreword

The October Gallery is delighted to present this first book on the work of the artist El Anatsui, which has been made possible by an Arts Council award under the *Artists' First Time Publications* scheme. In 1993 when we first exhibited the work of El Anatsui and before we began to represent his interests world-wide, we were acutely aware that, for an African artist with a growing international reputation, there was no significant publication giving an insight into the artist himself and his sources of inspiration or that made a critical assessment of his work. This book, published on the occasion of his second solo exhibition at the Gallery, *A Sculpted History of Africa* (Spring 1998), addresses this situation.

The book includes sections in four major languages in order to give better access to Anatsui's work to the many peoples throughout the world who speak those languages and in countries where his reputation continues to grow.

Since his first major appearance on the international art stage as one of five artists representing Africa at the Venice Biennale in 1990, and the subsequent presentation of his work in London, New York, Tokyo, Washington, and at the Havana and Johannesburg Biennales, El Anatsui has become a leading force in contemporary art from Africa.

We hope that this book, by highlighting El Anatsui's contribution to the developing history of the *transvangarde*, will further contribute to the Gallery's objective of promoting vibrant contemporary art from around the planet.

I would like to express my gratitude to Elisabeth Lalouschek, Artistic Director of the October Gallery, who combines an ever-deepening knowledge of contemporary African art with a unique artistic *ésprit*, without her constant endeavours El Anatsui's work would not be so well-known today; to Gerard Houghton, wordsmith, who helped to assure the clarity and accuracy of three of the four languages in this work; to John Picton who brings charm, common sense and precision to a formidable understanding of

African Art; to Elizabeth Péri-Willis who has traced the significant threads of El Anatsui's influences; to Yukiya Kawaguchi who introduced El Anatsui to Japan and whose essay looks at his work from the perspective of another ancient culture; and to Simon Njami who, as editor of *Revue Noire*, continues to demonstrate so eloquently, to the French speaking world, the power and importance of contemporary African art.

The October Gallery especially acknowledges the unflagging support of Sajid and Shirley Rizvi of Saffron Books, Eastern Art Publishing, our partners in this venture, who hold fast to their vision of publishing books that are as necessary as they are beautiful; and the generosity of Agnes Zauner and the excellent staff at Amica Fine Art Printers, without whose commitment to quality and attention to detail this book would not have been so attractively finished nor in such record time.

We also extend wholehearted thanks to the Trustees and the dedicated staff of the October Gallery; to Dr. Johanna Lalouschek (who proof-read the German text); to Patricia Tehami (who proof-read the French text and translated El Anatsui's quotations into French); to Karen Boston, doctoral student at the Courtauld Institute and to Sandor Péri for support and liaison with El Anatsui in Nigeria.

Finally, a word of special thanks to **africa95** for their support of the *Sculpted History of Africa* exhibition and to the British Council who continue to assist the October Gallery's work in so many different parts of the world, and who made it possible for El Anatsui to be in London on the occasion of the launch of this book.

— Chili Hawes
Director October Gallery

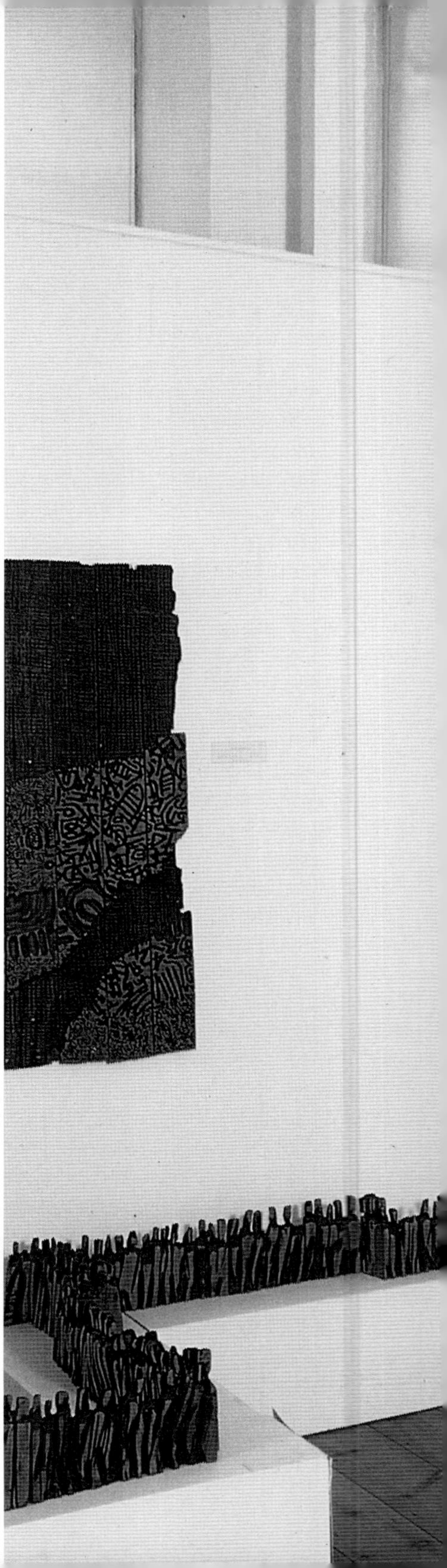

The October Gallery's 1995 exhibition by El Anatsui, including Erosion and Visa Queue

Photo: Andy Keate

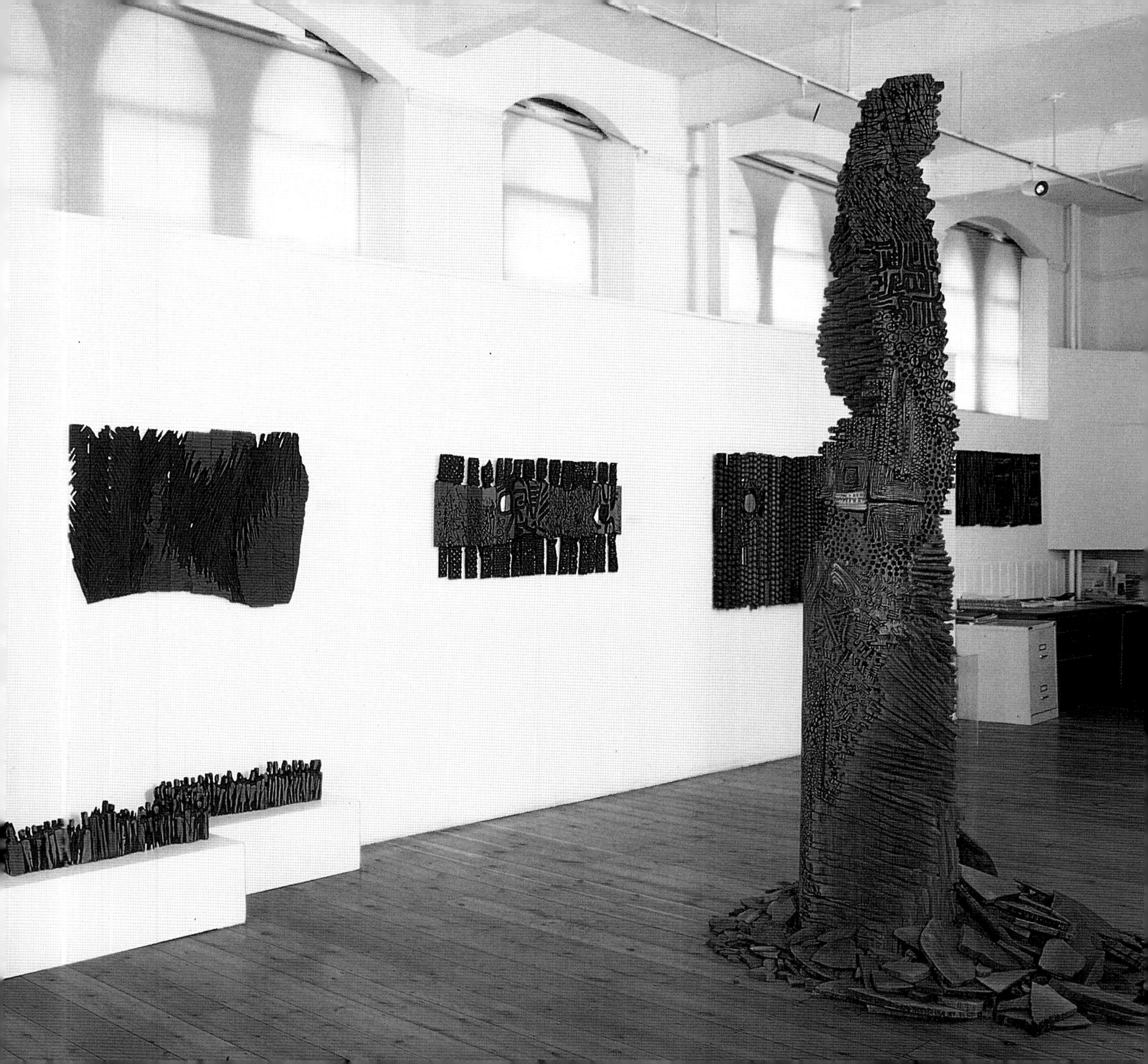

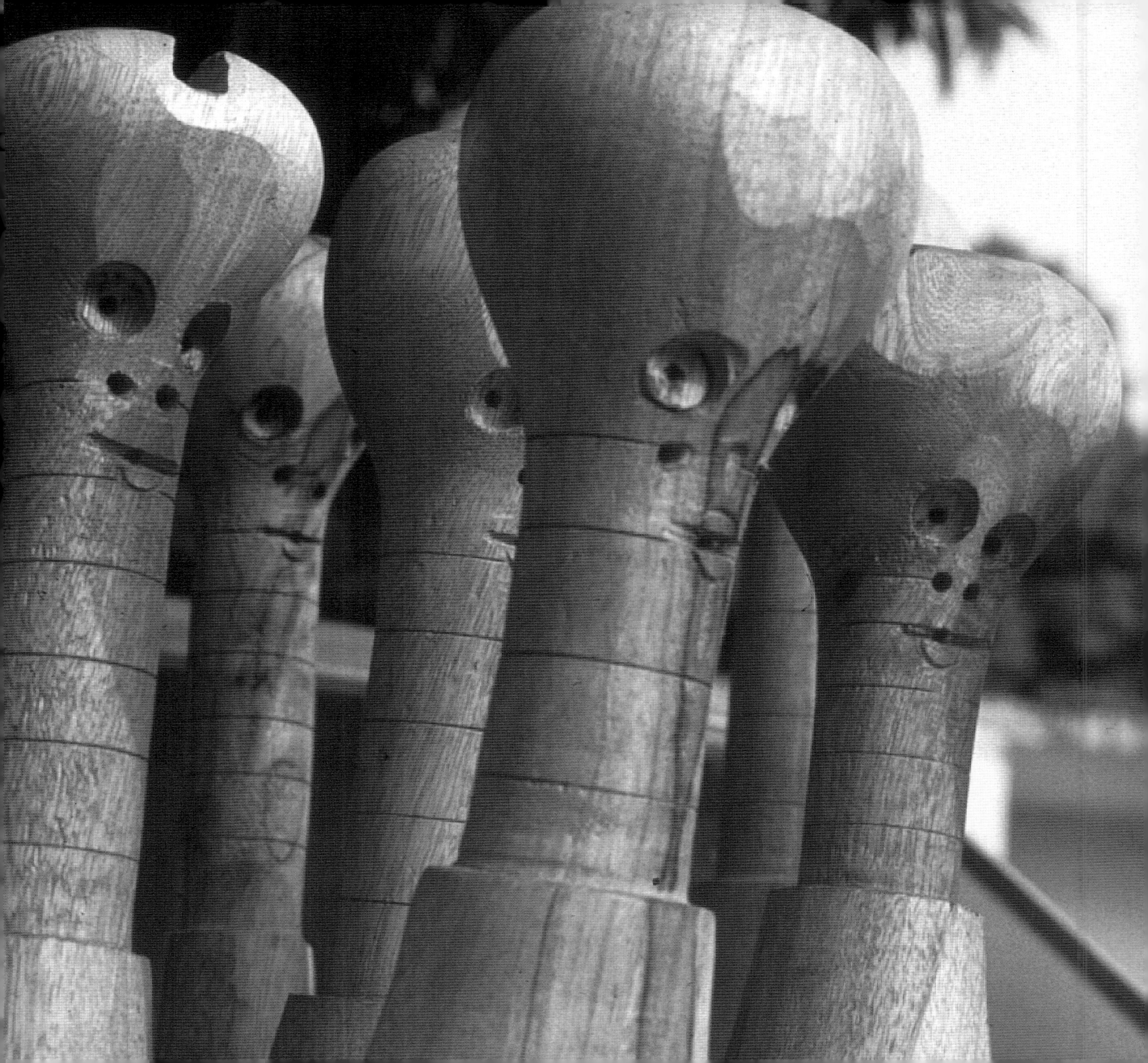

JOHN PICTON

'Patches of history' patching up my art history: some reflexions on the sculpture of El Anatsui, 1998

Harlem, Venice, Nsukka

I was introduced to the sculpture of El Anatsui by the 1990 Venice Biennale. I write this with no particular sense of achievement: rather, if anything, the opposite. Having supposed myself to have a measure of expertise in the field of West African art, and of Nigerian art in particular, I was covered with confusion to discover an artist with whose work I was not at all familiar. At that time El Anatsui had been living and working in Nigeria for fifteen years, at one of the country's most significant university fine art teaching departments. He had already achieved an international reputation, and had been among the artists featured in Kojo Fosu's monumental *20th Century Art of Africa*[1], published in Nigeria four years previously. One had no excuse, no matter how well informed one had previously thought oneself to be; and I cite my 'introduction' here for the manner in which it stands as an index of the extent of the continuing level of ignorance about art practice in sub-Saharan Africa contemporary with our time. The resilience of the *'Myth of Primitivism'*[2] is deeply disturbing; and it thus still has much to answer for, including the often unwitting collusion between that 'primitivism' and (a certain kind of now rather old-hat) museum ethnography. This collusion serves to institutionalise an art world for Africa from which many of the developments in recent and contemporary practice are excluded; and it was for this precise reason that the African presence at

[1] Fosu, K, 1986, *20th Century Art of Africa,* Zaria: Gaskiya Corporation [Artists Alliance, Accra], 2nd ed, 1993.

[2] Hiller, S, ed, *The Myth of Primitivism: Perspectives on Art,* London and New York: Routledge, 1991.

Devotees, 1987

variable installation, black afara

height 34cm, width 43cm, depth 30cm

John Picton is Reader in African Art, Department of Art and Archaeology, SOAS, University of London. From 1961 to 1970, he worked in Nigeria for the Federal Government Department of Antiquities and thereonward till 1979 at the British Museum. His research interests include Yoruba and Benin sculpture; masquerade; textile history and 20th century development of the visual arts in Africa. For africa95, *he was consultant/co-curator of* Technology, Tradition and Lurex: The Art of African Textiles *at the Barbican Centre (September-December 1995). He also contributed to the catalogue of the exhibition,* Africa: The Art of a Continent *(Royal Academy, October 1995-January 1996, and other venues); and was a speaker at both* African Artists: School, Studio and Society *(SOAS conference, September 1995) and* Eastern Art Report*'s conference,* Myths and Mothballs *(Courtauld Institute, October 1995). He is currently working on two publications in Saffron Books' African Art and Society series, based on the proceedings of a SOAS/October Gallery conference on* Visual Art in Post-Apartheid South Africa, *held in June 1996, and the SOAS/October Gallery conference on the Yoruba Diasporas in 1997.*

the 1990 Venice Biennale really was something of an international breakthrough.

The significance of the 1990 Biennale for 20th century art in Africa was twofold. It was the first time the work of artists from sub-Saharan Africa had been included. (Subsequent biennales have continued to show work from sub-Saharan Africa: from Senegal and from South Africa). Second, this was an exhibition prepared by Grace Stanislaus, then of the Studio Museum in Harlem, and the significance of this African American location and of its curator should not be overlooked. In preparing the 1990 Venice Biennale exhibition Grace Stanislaus drew upon the research for her *Contemporary African Artists: Changing Traditions* show at the Studio Museum in Harlem earlier that year, an exhibition that remains still among the best accounts of its subject.[3] (I am grateful to my friend and colleague Elsbeth Court for telling me about the Venice and Harlem exhibitions and pay tribute to the efficiency of her information gathering, and her generosity in sharing it with those who would otherwise remain in ignorance).

[3]Stanislaus, G [et al], *Contemporary African Artists: Changing Traditions*, New York: Studio Museum in Harlem, 1990.

In Venice as in Harlem, there was another artist, Bruce Onobrakpeya, with whose work I certainly was familiar, having known him since the 1960s when I too worked in Lagos. Yet, as certainly, I knew nothing of the relationship between these two artists as mediated by Uche Okeke, that singular genius in the history of art in Nigeria during the latter half of the present century. I write this not in any sense to disparage the work of either Onobrakpeya or Anatsui but simply to identify Okeke as an artist who, by common consent, must be reckoned among the most significant catalysts for development in the visual arts in West Africa since the 1950s, especially in re-shaping the developments of a Modernism as initiated by Aina Onabolu (1882-1963).[4]

[4]Deliss, C [et al], *Seven Stories about Modern Art in Africa*, London: Whitechapel Art Gallery, 1995.

Okeke and Onobrakpeya had been students together from 1958 to 1961 at the first tertiary-level fine art department in Nigeria, the incipient Ahmadu Bello University in Zaria. Natural Synthesis was the dominant idea, that synthesis of the media learned through formal education with the artist's own experiences, whether local or international, and especially including the formal traditions each artist inherits and draws upon from his or her own past. Rather than resolving into a narrow-minded ethnic or cultural nationalism, Natural Synthesis led to the recognition that one could be Igbo and Nigerian, Yoruba and Nigerian, Edo and Nigerian, and so forth, that these differences could be celebrated in the interests of the unity and identity of a Nigeria that was independent of colonial rule.

Onabolu's principal achievements had been, first, to show that Africans were not to be constrained by the 'myth of primitivism,' that they could paint pictures as well as anyone else; second, to bring about the inception of art education within British colonial education in Africa; and third, to document and commemorate through portraiture the leading Nigerians of his time. In this context Okeke's Natural Synthesis was a 'vital and enabling' development.[5]

[5]Appiah, K A, *In My Father's House*, London: Methuen, 1992, p293.

Among the influences upon Uche Okeke was a drawing tradition that owed nothing to Europe, the seemingly obsolescent tradition of body and mural painting known as *uli*, which he had learned something about from his mother. In 1975, in an era of post-civil-war reconstruction, Okeke and Anatsui became colleagues in the fine art department of the University of Nigeria, Nsukka (founded by President Nnamdi Azikiwe at the time of Independence as the first university in the country to award its own degrees).

Okeke as head of a reconstituted post-civil-war department instituted research into *uli*, encouraging students to investigate this art in their home villages, and thereby encouraging a certain spirit of form and line in the work of his department. This was the cultural environment in which El Anatsui, arriving from Ghana, now found himself, and to which he brought a familiarity with traditions of visual practice in sculpture, metal-casting, mural decoration, textile design and so forth, that were very different from anything he would find around Nsukka, and yet the two sets of traditions could be brought together.

The first part of this particular narrative, concerning the relationship between Onobrakpeya and Okeke, I knew quite well, having arrived in Nigeria within the first year of Independence; but I knew nothing of the second part, the relationship between Anatsui and Okeke. So, confronted with his work in 1990, what did I see? The work on show at the Venice Biennale comprised nine groups of wooden panels placed together edge to edge and carved, burned, painted and lacquered. With titles such as *Left me with half an identity*, or *Long before the chief executives started telling us, the surest way of getting water is prayers.* I knew enough to grasp something of the manner in which issues of immediate and continuing significance were being addressed in ways that also entailed referrals to certain traditions of visual practice inherited from the past. Knowing something about textiles in West Africa certainly helped,[6] even if I was unable to realise the full complexity of the synthesis before me, and especially El Anatsui's engagement with *uli* and also *nsibidi* (a tradition of graphic signs associated with the Leopard Society of the Cross River region) in addition to the graphic signs hand printed on Asante *adinkra* cloths.[7]

[6] Picton, J [et al], *The Art of African Textiles: Technology, Tradition and Lurex*, London: Lund Humphries Publishers, 1995.

[7] Ottenberg, S, *New Traditions from Nigeria: Seven Artists of the Nsukka Group*, Washington DC: Smithsonian Institution Press, 1997. The most authoritative recent study done on this group of artists.

However, while in 1990 I needed to know much more to grasp the full range of implications of El Anatsui's work, I would not wish to suggest either that artworks are in any sense necessarily the prisoners of their originary circumstances, or that the artists somehow have proprietary rights over the interpretation of their work. A concern with the history of a piece and a respect for the artist obliges us, of course, to understand as much as we can about these things; but it does not prescribe them alone as the only privileged and authentic basis of our engagement with that work. The capacity of any work of art to withstand, perhaps even to encourage, explanations, understandings and conceptions that transcend its origins (as if the work itself had a life of its own) is among the more disconcerting attributes of art. Yet it is precisely this capacity that imparts continuing relevance to the work.

Memory, Imagination, Art

The book for which this essay is written is about a man who is a sculptor, about the forms that are shaped by his hands, and about the ideas and memories presupposed and inherent in those forms; but just what is this 'in'? It is all very well for an artist to refer to his work, as El Anatsui sometimes does, as some kind of container of memory, thereby perhaps intending us to assume an analogy between the work of art and the human brain, or rather the brain within its skull (as if the skull were like the artwork); but the relationships between ideas and practices are by no means simple matters. Nor can these relationships somehow be taken for granted. (Another artist from Nigeria, Osi Audu, has taken to referring to his own artwork in terms of the idea of the 'inner head' as publicised through the research and writing of the contemporary Yoruba scholarship centred on Obafemi Awolowo University, Ile-Ife, where Audu had been a student, and where he had been taught by one of the leading exponents of these ideas, Rowland Abiodun).[8]

[8] Abiodun, R; H J Drewal; J Pemberton, *Yoruba: Art and Aesthetics in Nigeria*, Zürich: Museum Rietberg, 1991.

Works of art neither think nor talk even if they incorporate words within their forms. (This is something which, in Africa, is particularly beloved of the so-called popular artists, such as Cheri Samba of Kinshasa, or Kwame Akoto of the Almighty God Artworks, Kumasi, artists who emerge from the sign-painting traditions adopted during the time of colonial rule. These artists have sometimes been described as 'auto-didacts,' ie essentially self-taught, and thus free of the inhibitions of the academy. Aside from this as merely yet another insidious regression to the 'myth of primitivism,' it is factually quite wrong. The artists working within the sign-painting tradition are in

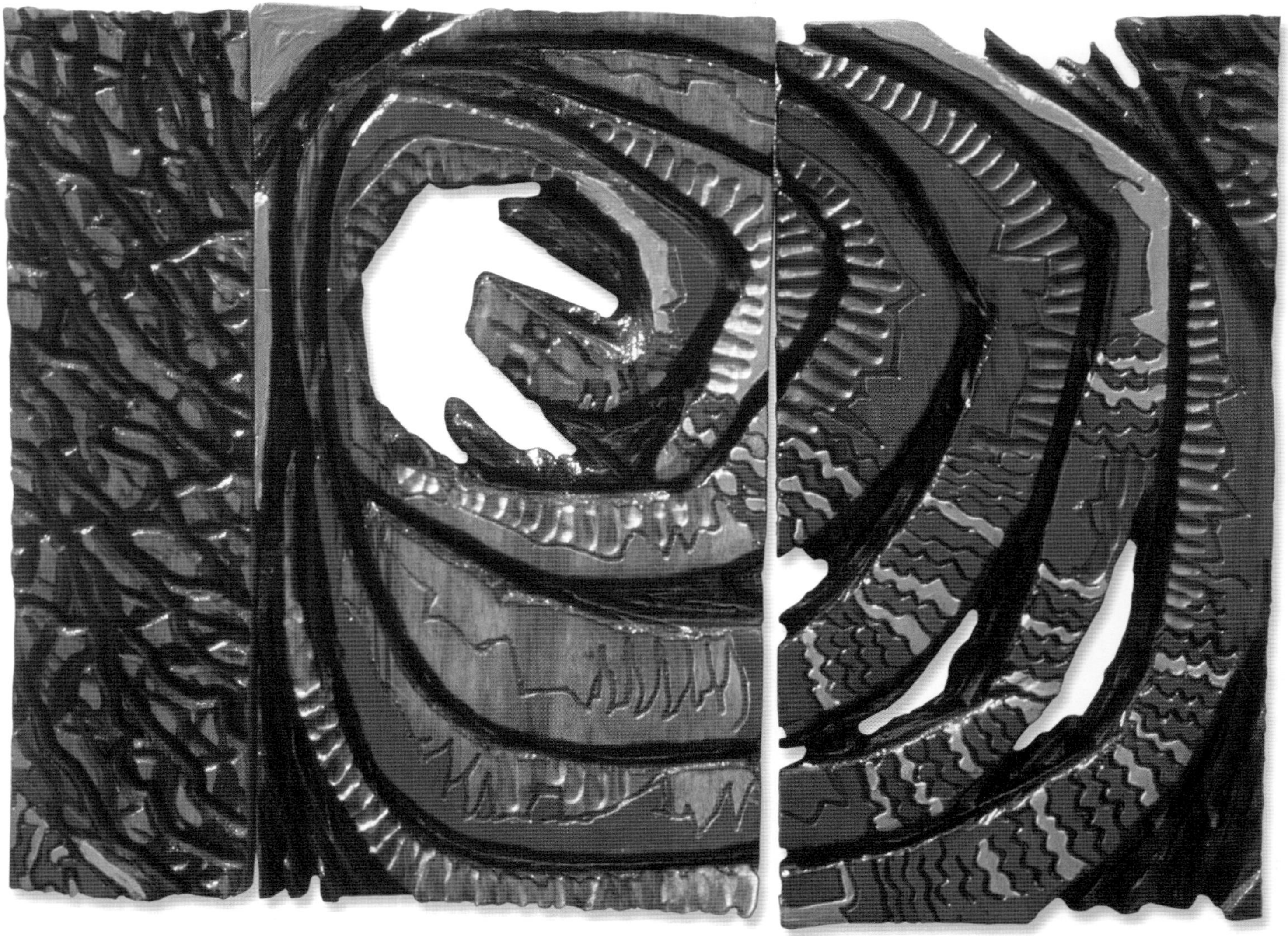

Agwolagwo (Coils of the Python), 1988

wood relief, tropical hardwoods
height 84cm, width 102cm & depth 4cm

Photo: El Anatsui

reality trained by a system of apprenticeship far more rigorous in its manner of direction than anything that happens in a university fine art studio. Sign painting, like motor mechanics, has become the subject of indigenous didactic tradition alongside — where they continue to flourish - hand-loom weaving, wood sculpture, brass-casting, and so forth).

Moreover, works of art only move if they are deliberately kinetic, as in the work of Sokari Douglas-Camp. For there is nothing in a work of art in any literal sense other than what is physically there (I accept, of course, that local theories of art may presuppose and take for granted the presence of animate properties, but that is a separate issue which, in any case, does not bear upon the concern with memory). Whether the work of art is taken as signifying realities beyond itself, or as signifying the thing that it is in itself, this remains true if only because of the sociality (the social-ness if you prefer) that is always inevitable about art, notwithstanding the individuality of its maker. (The artist is, indeed, part of the constitution of that social world).

Neither do works of art do anything, nor are they for anything (in particular), and yet all social life is in significant ways predicated upon art. For we do lots of things with and in terms of art: we entertain ourselves; we heal ourselves; we enact and enable our social networks, networks without which we have virtually no possibilities of existence; we mark things out; we codify our dreams, imaginations, aspirations, hopes; we grasp at realities that are literally beyond our grasp; and so on and so forth. In all of this works of art are, as I have suggested, both things and signs. Perhaps it is worth recalling that the very notion of theory depends upon the faculty of sight. (The word theory itself derives from the Greek for sight).[9]

[9] Williams, R, *Keywords,* London: Fontana, 1976.

> Memory, according to the ancient Greeks, was the precondition of thought. The art of memory, as it was practiced in the ancient world, was a pictorial art, focusing not on words but on images. It treated sight as primary. It put the visual first. Outward signs were needed if memories were to be retained and retrieved.[10]

[10] Samuel, R, *Theatres of Memory,* London and New York: Verso, 1994, vii-viii.

This might seem to contradict the thrust of this part of my essay; but in reality it points us towards the dependence of art and of our understanding of it on context and projection. Art is social and it is also autonomous; and that autonomy almost inevitably imparts a hermetic quality. As a physical object there is nothing there that is not physically there, but we do not readily see art or think of art in quite that hard-headed way. As Wollheim pointed out twenty years ago, we have learned to talk about and see qualities in a work of art that cannot possibly be there, and yet those very fictitious qualities are vital to our understanding of the work in question.[11] It is we who do the putting in, not through some kind of essentially inherent presence, but through the imaginary project that art is also. We invest the artefact with mnemonic properties. We act as if objects could act, and as if they could contain our powers of recollection. We project life, as if we could 'see' the capacity to permit recall, enabling us to imagine the work as a container of memory; we project a narrative of events and dreams, of communities and individuals, of interpretations and ideologies, histories of several kinds if you like; and we project ideas of being the same as (and different from) others in terms of the artwork.

[11] Wolhein, R, *Art and Its Objects,* New York: Harper & Row, 1968, and reprinted several times, most recently 1992, by the Cambridge University Press, England.

Then, it becomes possible to consider the extent to which these memories, entailed or provoked in any process of art-making, can be transferred via the artwork to its viewers? If we have the art-historical documents together with the discourse of the artist, then we might, maybe; but what if we do not? The best we can hope for is that any artwork is invested (by us) with the power to evoke other memories, ideas that were never part of the originary circumstances and significances. Without some knowledge of West African textiles, El Anatsui's work at the 1990 Venice Biennale would have looked like flat pieces of wood; and there can be no guarantee that in the absence of his own discourse anything of his ideas and memories as embedded through his personal experiences can be carried across. Yet the idea that El Anatsui presents a series of memorials to and recollections of his life experiences is a powerful idea. It moves us to want to know more of the history and context of his art making; and it seems to me to be of especial significance, in the life history of this one artist, as in the 20th-century history of art in sub-Saharan Africa, that we look to the sources and resources drawn upon by artists.

For when we do, we do not find that break between past and present so beloved of that consortium of the 'myth of primitivism' and old-hat museum ethnography (and I do not intend to condemn all ethnography and social anthropology, only the slipshod applications thereof) that has created the insidious category of 'traditional' art as the one authentic locus of all that really matters about art in Africa.[12] The idea of tradition on the other hand, that process of 'handing over' which inevitably entails the possibilities and actualities of change, even in the very idea of replication, is far more subtle. For the history of art has always depended on the inheritance of the past just as it has always been a narrative of loss and gain. That inheritance is not rejected by that generation of artists who emerge in the light of Independence from colonial rule, nor by those who come after; but it is an inheritance that is, as art work always has been, re-worked, re-presented, re-directed, transformed, within a context that is also part and parcel of those processes of change and development. The idea of tradition is fundamental in art as in social life, and not just in Africa. El Anatsui, Uche Okeke, Bruce Onobrakpeya and the others are not simply the products of an education system instituted to serve the demands of colonial rule; for that education contained the reasons for the demise of that colonialism; and meanwhile if their parents and other of their close kin were not artists, the skills of local hands were everywhere to be seen.

Understanding the projection of ideas and experiences 'into' and 'through' works of art thus also depends upon the idea of 'context,' that ever-present metaphor of social practice derived from the process of weaving (Latin *texere* to weave). Now weaving depends upon the interlacing of two sets of elements to produce thereby a coherent fabric. In that sense, works of art are themselves contexts ('weavings together') of ideas-and-practices. Equally, of course, works of art participate in contexts ('weavings together') of ideas-and-practices with the additional capacity imparted to its constituent artefacts of standing for those contexts. Remove the artwork from its originary circumstances and little of the ideas associated with it may be transferred; and even after painstaking research, all that is possible may be no more that an assumed reconstruction. This is no less true of the mnemonic contents of El Anatsui's work notwithstanding his status within the international art world, than it is of those countless works that commemorate the deceased in one tradition after another in Africa, as also in those works that are overtly intended to provide some kind of record of events.[13]

Yet the work that survives from one generation to another is precisely that work that can allow multiple and successive understandings, that will take a 're-writing' of its contextual associations, that will permit novel projections upon itself. El Anatsui may liken his artworks to 'chambers of memory;' but artworks last longer than their makers, and no one interpretation can be considered as necessarily privileged, not even that supplied by the artist. It is possible that the general mnemonic idea will be all that is passed on. El Anatsui's memories comprise the 'vital and enabling' (Appiah again)[14] engine that drives his art making, such that, together with sources of design that are both new and old, and technical means likewise, work is done that is strong enough to receive the memories and dreams of successive viewers who will make such sense of his work as they prefer,

[12]Picton, J (ed), *Image and Form: Prints, Drawings and Sculpture from southern Africa and Nigeria*, School of Oriental and African Studies, University of London, 1997.

[13]Mack, J, *Emil Torday and the Art of the Congo*, London: British Museum, 1990; Ravenhill, P, *Dreams and Reverie*, Washington DC: Smithsonian Institution Press, 1996; Roberts, M N & A F, *Memory: Luba Art and the Making of History*, New York: Museum for African Art, 1996; Wolfe, E, D Parkin and R Sieber, Vigango: The Commemorative Sculpture of the Mijikenda, Bloomington: University of Indiana Press, 1981.

[14]Appiah, K A, *In My Father's House*, London: Methuen, 1992.

always remembering that his own ideas about his work are also there to be drawn upon, or not, as people choose the manner in which they place their own memories within the containers that he has prepared for them, and place themselves in relation to one another thereby.

What is Africa to Me? That Vital and Enabling Badge(?)[15]

So, this essay and the book for which it is written are about a man who is a sculptor and about the forms that are shaped by his hands. It is also, thereby, about a history of art, and about Africa; but as with the question of what is 'in' a work of art, the question what is 'Africa' is by no means a simple matter either. Neither can it somehow be taken for granted that 'Africa' is the label an artist like El Anatsui actually needs.

Africa: a continent of snow and sunshine, of forest and desert, of rainfall and drought; of earth, air, fire and water, of gold and diamonds, of palm oil and petroleum, of saints as well as (such is the tragedy of the human condition) slaves; a continent with a longer human history than any other, a continent from which modern people emerged some half a million years ago to inhabit the whole world and paint pictures of it; a continent in which, as a result, there is greater genetic diversity than in any other. What, however, are the implications of all this for art? For there is neither an obvious nor a necessary fit between genetic and social inheritance (and I do take it for granted that all those things we call 'art,' visual, material, poetic, performance, must be included within and as part of the constitutions of social worlds). The one is not predicated upon the other: hence the illusion of race, that fiction based upon an ignorance of genetics that yet has had the ideological power to drive racism; and racism certainly is as real as it is pernicious and persistent.

Indeed, a triple legacy of slavery, the colonialism that replaced it, and the racism underpinning both, has constituted an Africa that has been perhaps the most misunderstood continent in the world. Not that any of these is a simple matter either: one remembers, for example, as if the horrors and brutalities of transatlantic slavery were not enough, that slaving also proceeded across the Sahara, down the Nile and across the Indian Ocean. Moreover, British colonial rule was undoubtedly almost benign when compared with King Leopold's viciously named 'Congo Free State.' So it is with some sense of relief that one learns that mediaeval Islamic travel writers wrote of sub-Saharan Africa in the most glowing terms, as though its kingdoms were paragons of ordered civilisation, or that Portuguese connoisseurs of the time around 1500 were prepared to pay substantial import duties for West African carved ivories, and a painter depicted Mary kneeling on Kongo plaited raphia fabric to receive the angel's message.[16] Indeed, the evidence for the antiquity of African technological innovation (and not just in ancient Egypt, for there were, for example, already Black potters in what became the central Sahara long before the formation of pre-dynastic civilisation) and for mercantile activities is now incontrovertible.

The fragmenting of Africa into 'tribes' and 'cultures' (and even into nation states) is substantially a consequence of a 'modern' world. This was constituted in a European prosperity from the 16th century onwards that was itself based upon the cheap labour, materials and goods provided by enslaved and colonised peoples. This was a process of fragmentation that provided strategies for the control of enslaved Africans in the Americas as well as for the administration of colonial territories in Africa; and this fragmenting is also, like racism, both persistent and pernicious for the very reason that it has served to deny the realities of the histories of social practice in Africa which, as far as one can tell, have always been constituted in that complex inter-relationship between local and global elements.[17] We can perceive this fragmentation most obviously in the classification of African artworks into their 'tribal' designations, or with African art in general into the contrast between

[15] Cullen, C, *Heritage (1925)*, reprinted in H L Gates Jnr & N Y McKay [eds], *African American Literature*, London and New York: W W Norton, 1997, p1311, & Appiah, KA, 1992 op. cit.

[16] Bassani & Fagg, *Africa and the Renaissance*, The Center for African Art, New York, 1988.

[17] Fardon, R (ed), *Counterworks*. London and New York: Routledge, 1995.

'traditional' and 'contemporary' (and while both terms have their validity, in the traditional/contemporary paradigm, valid usage is misconstrued).[18] We can also perceive it in the way Africa is to be found in the several departments of an institution such as the British Museum: the prehistoric, mediaeval, oriental, Egyptian, Greek and Roman, ethnographic, and prints departments all have African material, yet this material is nowhere brought together, nor is there any intention so to do. Of course, it can be argued that the Afrocentric quest (so beloved of African Americans, with real justification — though it would take a long time to explain why) for an African unity is mere wishful thinking; but like everything else, it is not quite as simple as one would like it to be. For there are bonds of continuity (as well as the evident discontinuities) across time and space that cannot be forgotten, even as they should not be invested with more power than they deserve.

Thus, the demographic pressures contingent upon the climatic changes that brought the Sahara into existence were felt along the Nile valley as well as in what is now the Sahel region. Much later, there was the distribution of a complex of elements, including iron-working and Bantu languages from the region that is now the border between Nigeria and Cameroon throughout much of eastern, central and southern Africa. Then there are the complex networks of trade, across the Sahara, across the Indian Ocean: Malian gold in Cairo, Mediterranean brass in ancient Ife, Chinese ceramics in Great Zimbabwe. Then Europeans begin their travels around the coast; but Africa had always been an international phenomenon. At the same time it must also be recognised that what stands as a bond of continuity for some stands as discontinuity for others. Even in the 19th century there were still places without an iron-working technology. The distribution of casting technologies is not universally located. Technologies, forms, styles, traditions, ideas, titles, languages, social formations, ritual practices, networks of trade: each has its particular history as traced in its distribution.

Nevertheless, there is a commonality about the experience of colonial rule, about the contesting thereof, and about the questions of identity that are entailed in these processes. For identities are real yet constructed. The modern sense of an Igbo identity, in the promulgation of which *uli* painting was incorporated, came about as a result of an internal diaspora within colonial Nigeria in which people looked back and saw common ground between them and people from the next village, town, group, and so forth.[19] For Igbo people this gave rise to the Igbo State Union, a political and cultural organisation. For Europeans, this gave rise to the Igbo tribe; and yet there never was any such thing. Of course, to raise the idea of identity is to risk the accusation of responsibility for yet more 'cliché-ridden discourse;'[20] but it is none the less an idea that is hard to avoid. For the subject of how some people are connected together while others are split apart, and of how art is entailed therein, is after all rather important, especially because of the details of local communal and individual action and agency (rather than because of the principals or generalities asserted in the relevant literature).

In terms of the ethnographic conventions of the past El Anatsui would be described as Ewe, that ethnic identity located in south-eastern Ghana and southern Togo, an identity that in fact emerges only towards the end of the 19th century as a result of, and in response to, northern German missionary activities. Ewe communities are perhaps best known for their traditions of narrow-strip weaving (located in Kpetoe, Keta, and elsewhere; and the subject of current research by Malika Kraamer of the School of Oriental and African Studies, University of London).

One can certainly see the trace of this in El Anatsui's work, as already noted, although as it happens he was trained in the fine art department of the University of Science and Technology in Kumasi, the capital city of the confederation of kingdoms that were brought together about 1700 to form the Asante nation. Not far from Kumasi are the villages of Bonwire, Ntonso and Wonoo, each also subsisting considerably on the weaving (and in the case of Ntonso, the hand-printing) of textiles,

[18] Picton, J, 'Desperately Seeking Africa,' *Oxford Art Journal* 15, 2, pp104-112, Oxford University Press, 1992.

[19] Willis, E A, *Uli Painting and Identity: Twentieth Century Developments in Art in the Igbo-speaking Region of Nigeria*, University of London, PhD thesis, 1997, pp237-239.

[20] Appiah, K A & and H L Gates jnr [eds], *Identities*, Chicago and London: University of Chicago Press, 1995.

superficially very like those woven by Ewe people, though markedly different in ways that once seen are not easily forgotten. Textile production, therefore, is only one among many visual art traditions that can be presumed to have become embedded in the experiences El Anatsui brings to his sculpture.

Moving then to the University of Nigeria, Nsukka, to take up a teaching appointment he encountered Okeke's Natural Synthesis together with all the wealth of visual practice available through the communities and museums of Nigeria. Should we call El Anatsui an Ewe sculptor? Or perhaps, because of his use of *uli*, he is now an Igbo sculptor? or perhaps we have to be a little more subtle, asking instead what are the circumstances (if any) in which these labels have any significance at all? Sometimes it seems as if we can only look at Africa backwards and through a cracked looking-glass; and, in certain circumstances, even 'African' may become uncomfortable as a label. El Anatsui's work can now be found across at least four continents, in Japan, West Africa, Britain and elsewhere in Europe, and in the National Museum of African Art, Washington DC.

In the 1990 Venice Biennale, Great Britain was represented by Anish Kapoor (who, born in Bombay, lives and works in London), of whom Thomas McEvilley wrote:

> Kapoor's ambiguous placement in history is part of the premise of the work. There is a paradoxical challenge to the situation of a colonial practising Modernism. Modernism was an ideology that incorporated India, and of course many other places, as fixtures of empire, not sources from which new expressions of cultural identity — British cultural identity! — might arise.[21]

[21]McEvilley, T, Great Britain, in *General Catalogue 1990, La Biennale di Venezia,* pp182-183 [Catalogue Editor M-G Gervasoni], Milan: Fabri Editori, 1990.

To ask whether Anish Kapoor is Indian or British is to miss the point. To ask if El Anatsui is Ewe, Ghanaian, Nigerian, or whatever else, is, likewise, to miss the point. Apart from anything else, for them as for the rest of us, it all depends on the circumstances in which an identity must be identified.

> ...we can choose...what it will mean to be African in the coming years...it is really unsurprising that a continental identity is coming into cultural and institutional reality...We share a continent...we share a relation of dependency...we share the problem of racism...'African' can surely be a vital and enabling badge; but in a world of genders, ethnicities, classes and languages, of ages, families, professions, religions and nations, it is hardly surprising that there are times when it is not the label we need.[22]

[22]Appiah K A, *In My Father's House,* op cit.

It is instructive to place Kwame Anthony Appiah and El Anatsui (and, for that matter, Anish Kapoor) next to one another in our imagination, not that somehow they are comparable or equivalent. That would be yet more simple-mindedness. Rather they each illustrate the multiplicity of identities that converge, differently in each case, around each person, identities that will not be tied down, identities that resist the fragmenting strategies of a colonialising Europe. El Anatsui's sculpture is what it is in part because of a life that draws upon things that are thoroughly African. Yet in the context of the persistence in Europe of a 'myth of primitivism' it is hardly surprising that 'African' is not the label El Anatsui necessarily always requires.

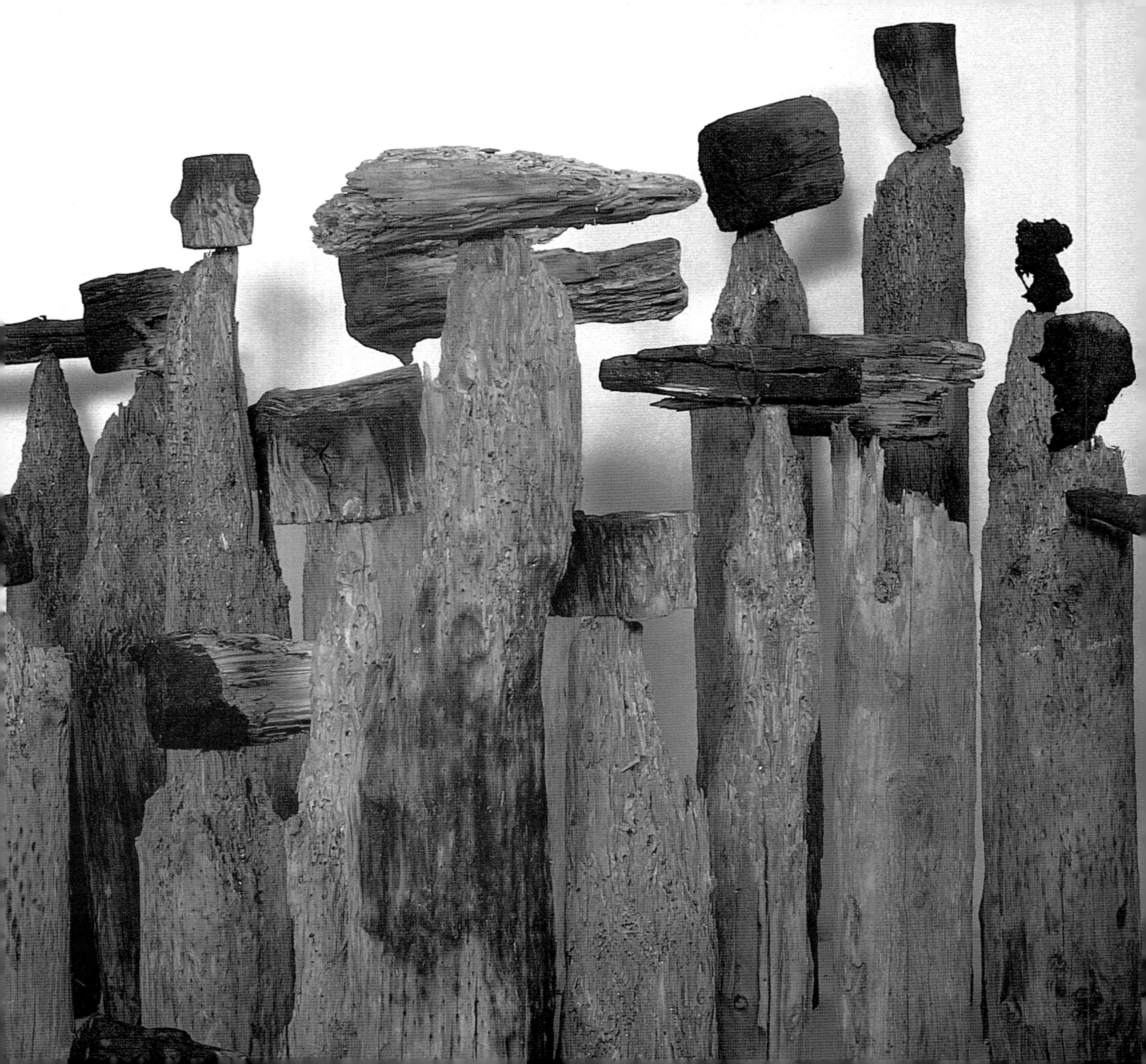

GERARD HOUGHTON

El Anatsui and the Transvangarde

The Transvangarde

This book, like the work of the artist that it celebrates, is a synthesis of the work of many people. In the West, we have become so used to considering the years of effort and discipline required to create a body of work as one of the distinguishing features of the artist *as individual* that it might come as a surprise in introducing El Anatsui, to situate him in relation to all those others implicated in his art. Yet perhaps this is not so wrong as at first it might appear. For the artist is never really, as we sometimes pretend, a solitary individual struggling in profound isolation. Rather, he is an individual engaged in a developing dialogue with the group of which he is a member, the successive levels of community because of which he exists and for whom he creates. El Anatsui himself makes explicitly clear that his work has both its source and its focus in other people and indeed in many other *groups* of people. These source groups might include: his family, his people, his teachers and the various other artists (both his peers and students — that level of community that is sometimes called a 'school') to whose common cause he contributes. The artist *as social being*, then, cannot honestly be separated from these many others any more than his work can exist without the sounding board of a receptive audience. Anatsui's art is about groups, about communities, about the migration of whole peoples across continents and

Akua's Surviving Children (detail), 1996

installation, found wood & metal

Photo: Andy Keate

Colour plate, pp38-39

Gerard Houghton was born in England. After receiving a Masters Degree from Churchill College, Cambridge in 1980, and travelling extensively throughout West Africa working as an interpreter for a researcher into African History, he took his considerable skills as a linguist to the East. As an Educational Advisor to the Kyoto Prefectural Government he has taught at all levels of the Japanese Education System, eventually being employed by the Japanese Ministry of Education to teach both Literature and Linguistics at the prestigious Kyoto University and Nara Women's University, Japan's longest established (1886) University for Women. A Graduate of the Urasenke School of Tea as well as a Licentiate of the Kameoka School of the Japanese Traditional Performing Arts, he has maintained a keen interest in Oriental Art since returning to the UK to join the October Gallery staff in 1995. He is a Director of the Institute of Ecotechnics, a London-based consultancy that advises on, develops and constructs ecological projects around the world.

about the intersecting histories of these various families, schools, peoples, nations and civilisations; and it is well, at the beginning of this first book devoted to his work, to be quite clear about these matters.

The particular historical circumstances that brought this book into being are anchored in El Anatsui's second solo exhibition at the October Gallery, *A Sculpted History of Africa* (Spring 1998). This London exhibition occurred at a time when his work was gathering more and more critical appreciation and international acclaim. Elisabeth Lalouschek, the October Gallery's Artistic Director, had begun to find herself ever more involved in transporting the work from Nigeria, to Germany, to England, to Japan, the States — and back again, rapidly having to master the co-ordination of complex transportation schedules from one overseas exhibition to the next. That a contemporary artist from Africa should be so sought after abroad lent strong support to an idea that the Gallery had long been promoting; but before progressing to ideas, perhaps a few relevant facts about the Gallery.

The October Gallery, just off Queen's Square and not far from the British Museum in Bloomsbury, was first conceived of in October, 1978, and opened its doors to the general public with an exhibition of the work of Gerald Wilde, the English Abstract Expressionist painter, early the following year. The Gallery was the brain-child of a creative group of international artists, musicians and actors who at the time were seeking a new European base for their wide-ranging artistic activities. The group understood that London, because of its geographical situation and its historical associations with so many different cultures, served as a major cross-roads for people from around the planet, and was fast becoming one of the world's truly multi-cultural cities. A London gallery, therefore, represented a prime cosmopolitan site from which to launch and develop an ongoing multi-cultural experiment in the visual arts.

Among the founder-members were three people who had established an architectural company, with whose help the group discovered and carefully restored a dilapidated three-storey Victorian school-building, which, from that time on, became the focal point of the London adventure. The intention, from the outset, was to create a home-from-home for artists and writers from other cultures; providing a congenial meeting-place where they could gather, connect and exchange ideas and a convenient exhibition space where they could show their work. The Gallery was to become a central point in a widespread network of creative individuals, offering a welcome to artists from far and wide, with each one contributing in his or her own way to the genius — and to the genesis — of the place. Among the many friends associated with the Gallery in those days were writers such as William S Burroughs, Tambimuttu, Lawrence Durrell, John Dolphin Allen and Ira Cohen, the artists Gerald Wilde, Brion Gysin and Marie Harding, the musicians Ornette Coleman, Kathelin Hoffman Gray and Keith Jarrett and many more besides. The vision and enthusiasm of artists such as these defined the initial direction that the Gallery took and has maintained to the present day. In the London of the late Seventies no other gallery was showing challenging art from around the world, and, though times have changed and the situation noticeably improved, the October Gallery still remains the only London gallery that consciously and consistently presents its audience with the work of original contemporary artists from the entire range of cultures around the globe.

From the outset the Gallery's artistic brief was simple: to exhibit and promote the work of the most exciting creative artists of the day — those who give substance and definition to the term 'cutting edge.' Mention of the 'cutting edge' in art leads, by a natural progression, to the idea of the *avant-garde*, yet, in this case, the association leads us astray. The word *avant-garde*, being used almost exclusively to describe artists of European and American provenance, makes less than adequate sense when discussing the work of contemporary African or Asian artists; 'Nigerian *avant-garde*,' for example, *sounds* like an oxymoron. Indeed this example reveals how much the received notion of *avant-garde* has become freighted with cultural assumptions that reinforce subconscious prejudices as to the primacy and importance of the western artistic tradition over any other. The reasons why this is the case are not hard to find. Western art has for so long written its own histories and preached its own virtues that it has begun to believe its own propaganda. Its self-appointed position of ascendancy over the creative productions of other peoples (bolstered by its control of the art market) has come to seem an incontrovertible fact. Within this closed loop of logic, *avant-garde* art (where it's really at!) is exclusively a western phenomenon!

Despite the frequent acknowledgement of 'borrowings' by European artists from the so-called 'primitive' traditions of Africa and Oceania, the consensus opinion still remains today that non-western cultures have contributed little or nothing to the western tradition of art. By extension, it is also often assumed that there are no 'contemporary artists' of any significance working outside the Euro-American tradition. It hardly needs to be said that this myopic appraisal results in a notion of Art (with a capital A) as limited as the restrictive categories applied in its formulation. Deeper reflection on the long history of cultural exchanges existing for so many centuries between Africa and Europe or Europe and the Orient, whereby materials, technologies and ideas were constantly passing from one to the other, would indicate that this supposedly pristine heritage is, in reality, an eclectic combination of elements and influences coming from a wide range of heterogeneous sources. If, therefore, one adopts at starting the truer position, that art is an activity common to all cultures and not the particular preserve of any single group or culture, then the world widens to become a richer realm of experience where 'art' is come upon in many unexpected forms and in all kinds of unsuspected places.

The Gallery's artistic focus aimed, from the outset then, to break beyond the barriers of the reductionist, Eurocentric position and advance into a new field that would embrace the finest contemporary work from any tradition and from all cultures. To help to define the goal of a gathering community of artists from all cultures who, through their art, are engaged in a frank exchange of cultural values and viewpoints, the better to communicate about essential questions of common concern to all, a new name was needed. With '*avant-garde*,' no longer appropriate, the word '*transvangarde*' was coined to indicate the less restrictive and more exciting notion of a *trans-cultural avant-garde*. The *transvangarde,* then, denotes a true vanguard of artists who, escaping from the limiting boundaries of their particular cultures begin to operate *between* and even *beyond* cultures. This becomes complex, but I would suggest that 'cultures' (such as the Welsh, Japanese, Basque, etc.) express only local sets of values beyond which it is possible — perhaps even desirable — to rise, to explore other levels of 'civilisations' (such as Greek, Yoruba, Egyptian, etc.), and beyond these, still wider levels of community. We are all, to take another example, representatives of a single species who inhabit the same delicately balanced biosphere. Who, if not the artists capable of a global vision, capable that is of transcending local culture and developing new and much-needed forms of global expression, is going to address and express matters of common concern to every culture at this, the widest level of community? The word '*transvangarde*' then is a shorthand way of indicating artists who emerging from one particular culture ultimately belong to all cultures equally, and

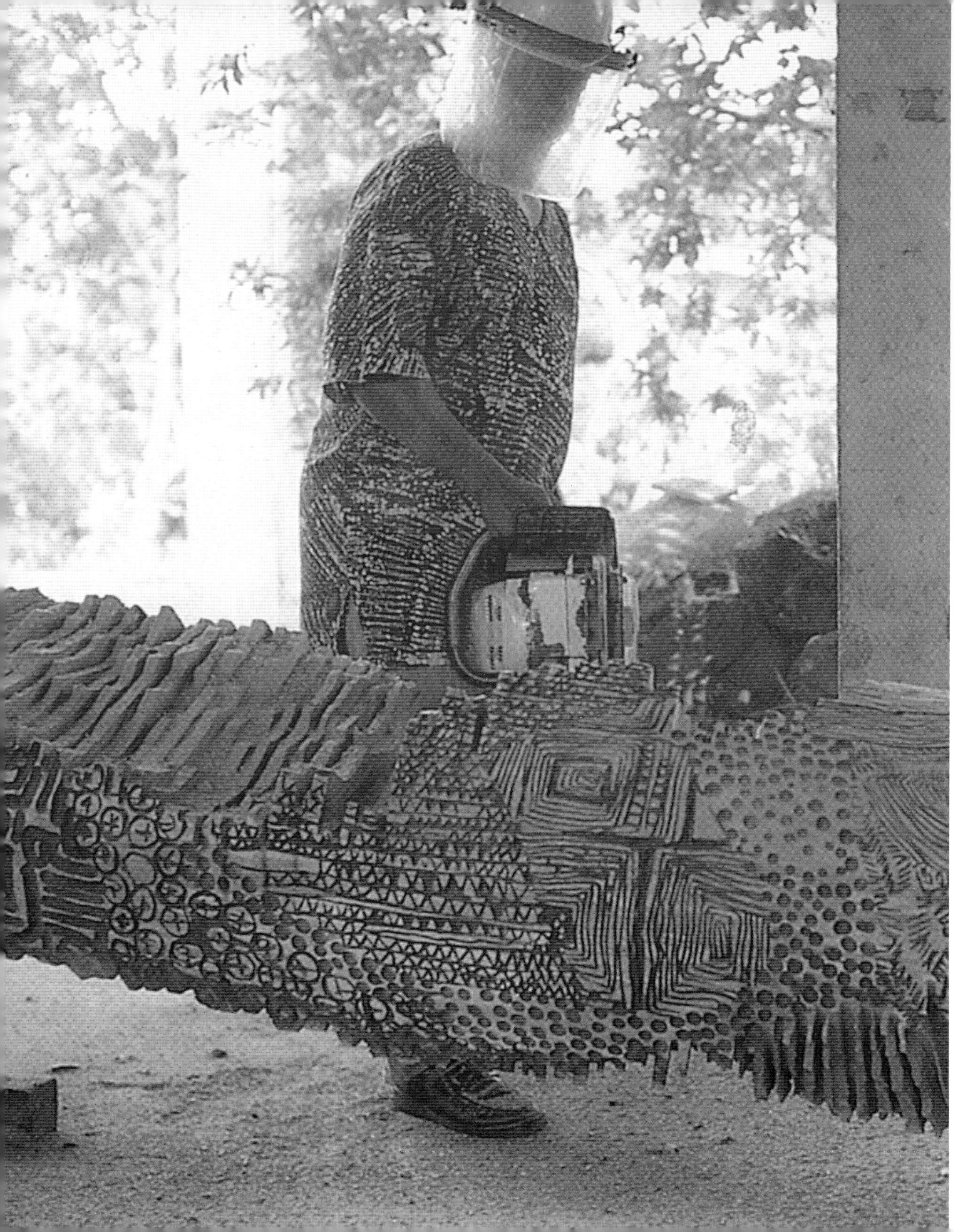

El Anatsui working on Erosion, *Brazil, 1992*

Photo: Miguel Rio Branco

are not to be described by culturally specific labels such as 'Ghanaian sculptor' or 'American painter'. They are trans-cultural artists — catalytic agents of the *transvangarde.*

In promoting this concept the October Gallery strives to identify and contact those global artists whose progressive work marks the leading edge of global contemporary art. During twenty years of exhibiting Painting, Sculpture and Photography from more than seventy different countries — the work of artists such as Aubrey Williams (Guyana), Kenji Yoshida (Japan), William S. Burroughs (USA), Ablade Glover (Ghana) and others — the Gallery has also curated a developing series of 'Transvangarde exhibitions' in which the work of two or more such artists is juxtaposed to create highly dramatic cross-cultural dialogues of visual thought-forms. It is in this context that the *transvangarde* can perhaps best be described as an ongoing multi-cultural experiment in the visual arts that is only to be understood in the context of a globally active — and consciously interactive — contemporary art scene without borders or boundaries.

El Anatsui

While issues arising from the fundamental imbalance of power written into relations between the west and the rest of the world have lately given pause to writers in Europe and America, the same issues have been the cause of extensive argument on the other side of the table over a much longer period. One can pick up the echoes of many such similar debates throughout Asia, Africa and Oceania during the postwar period, especially in the years leading up to and following each successive country's assertion of Independence from the colonial powers. For each of the newly-emergent States the rapid transition from a debilitating dependency to full autonomy raised a large number of difficult questions regarding the 'identity' of the new nation, eg: how 'modern' they were or wished to be? how best to govern themselves, giving expression to whatever indigenous cultures had survived the imprinting of the colonial years? etc. Such discussion was frequently of especial concern in the visual arts since it was often to the visual artists that a newly established national government would turn, commissioning them to create, out of the multi-cultural matrix, the visual cues and symbols that would help develop such fledgling feelings as national pride, a sense of national unity or purpose or indeed the complex construction of a whole, new, national identity.[1] Throughout this period, therefore, questions relating to the merits of indigenous artistic traditions as opposed to the assumed traditions of the west, the desirability of fostering hybridised modern traditions and so on were widely canvassed throughout Africa, since the answers to these and similar questions had ramifications at levels ranging from the personal through to the political.

Born in Ghana at the end of the war, El Anatsui was a young teenager at the time of Independence. While studying Art in Kumasi, at one of Africa's oldest Colleges of Art, he felt that the formal, academic training he was receiving — the syllabus still dominated by the legacy of Kumasi's strong ties with Goldsmith's College in London — was doing little to satisfy his own particular artistic inclinations. Dissatisfaction with this dry and, from an African perspective, inappropriate, western fare led him to seek out other stimuli, and he found inspiration in the bustling rural villages and colourful marketplaces. Here the productions of the local artisans, carvers and weavers, added to an already strong interest in the vibrant patterns of the Ewe and Asante cloths a fascination with other indigenous systems of pattern and design. In turning away from an imposed European aesthetic towards an older African sensibility Anatsui was perfectly in tune with his time. He records, in an interview,[2] how in post-Independence Ghana, visual and non-visual artists alike talked of a 'Go-back-and-pick'

[1] These problems and the use, by new governments, of artists as social engineers to draw together highly diverse tribal populations into a single nation have been repeated many times throughout the century. The case of Papua New Guinea, where the familiar struggle of indigenous artists to disregard western artistic expectations at the same time as they tried to determine an authentic 'national' style, as 'traditional' as it was 'modern,' makes for an interesting comparison. See Susan Cochrane's excellent account of this process , *Contemporary Art in Papua New Guinea*, Craftsman House, 1997.

[2] 'Sankofa: Go Back an' Pick. Three Studio Notes and a Conversation. El Anatsui,' *Third Text: Third world perspectives on contemporary art and culture*, Summer 1993, p48, London: Kala Press, 1993.

syndrome, meaning that they looked back to the pre-colonial past to try to re-discover and re-appropriate those elements of their own traditional artistic heritage that had been lost or become attenuated during the years of colonial rule.

A few years prior to the time that Anatsui was finding western art training so unappetising in Ghana, a small but highly motivated group of art students, led by Uche Okeke, in neighbouring Nigeria, had formed the Zaria Arts Society. This group was committed to a similar struggle, aiming to solve the contradictions of a contemporary Nigerian art based upon European stylistic conventions by rejecting the chronic copying of western forms in favour of the incorporation of design elements stemming from the many diverse Nigerian traditions. The Zaria Rebels, as they came to be known, campaigned for the recognition of an authentic Nigerian art based upon a 'Natural Synthesis'[3] of long established indigenous traditions, such as those of the Igbo, Yoruba and Hausa peoples, with whatever could usefully be adopted from the techniques and materials of the west. Interestingly, Okeke's idea was not simply to create a 'synthesis of old and new,' of indigenous and foreign forms, but included the notion that the distinctive traditions of the different peoples who now formed a new nation should each contribute its 'best' to a synthesis that would itself bring about a resurgence in Nigerian contemporary art. It must be remembered, here, that Nigerian art, with its two and a half millennia of continuous tradition, takes pride of place in sub-Saharan Africa for having, as Leopold Senghor once described it, 'the longest history and, therefore, the longest evolution.'[4] Okeke's eloquent championing of the latent, power of the African artist over what he perceived to be the uninspiring and dehumanised work of the 'modern machine-artist' of the west was based on more than mere rhetoric. He understood that if Nigerian contemporary art could successfully tap into the combined creativity of its pre-existent pool of cultures then the results would not only be a more powerful synthesis, but also a better reflection of the cultural diversity of the new nation, and thereby a better index of its true identity.

Okeke organised a sustained revaluation of the *uli* system of line drawing based on Igbo body and mural decorations, and the success of this single-minded quest to restore a tradition close to extinction can be seen both in his own work and the work of the many artists, (from various cultural backgrounds), who constituted a community of artists around him. The power of this idea and its catalytic effect upon this group of artists working together, changed the course of modern Nigerian art. What, however, is most interesting, is to see the way Okeke's own work achieves the 'synthesis' of which he spoke by bridging with such nimble ease the two divergent worlds of 'modern western' and 'traditional African.' Depending on ones view-point and familiarity with the different sources, when looking at Okeke's line drawings one can see them either as astoundingly *modern* portraits reminiscent of the finer moments of Picasso and Matisse, or as the quintessential distillation of *uli* abstract figurative technique. We have to pause, however, before applying words such as 'modern' or 'Picasso-esqe' to Okeke's line-drawings, and consider that what appears so familiarly 'modern' to us may actually be a conditioned response to an African aesthetic that we have learnt to associate with Picasso, but that *he* borrowed from African traditions of figurative abstraction to which Okeke's work stands in an even more direct relation still. The Andalusian, far from inventing the style we now call 'modern,' simply alerted the West to this other way of seeing. The man who diverted the course of modern western art owed more perhaps to Africa than the African who reshaped the course of modern Nigerian art owed to the West.

[3] Okeke, Uche, Natural Synthesis, 1960. Quoted in Okeke, Uche, *Art in Development — A Nigerian Perspective*, 1982, Asele Institute, Nimo Nigeria, Orion Printing Inc, USA.

[4] Senghor, Leopold Sedar, 1966, Address at the Premier Festival Mondial des Arts Negres, Dakar, Senegal.

When, in 1975, El Anatsui, moved from Ghana to take up a post in the Fine Arts Department of the University of Nigeria, Nsukka where Okeke was installed as Head of the Department, he found much in the approach of the older man to which he responded intuitively and with which he was immediately in tune. The move brought about a widening of artistic horizons and the added benefits of proximity to an excitingly different series of cultural traditions and influences, as well as the stimulus of finding himself within a community of artists, who each brought a different cultural background or individual perspective to the shared experiences of the Nsukka 'artistic family.' Besides the chance to research the *uli* figures in common with his new colleagues, Anatsui was able to explore the design strategies of *nsibidi*, the visually codified language of the Ekpé secret society with its rich allusions to proverbs and to local lore. He could also examine at first hand the rich traditions of Nigerian sculpture from the earliest Nok terracotta figures to the masterly Yoruba bronzes. It is Senghor again who reminds us that this diversity, a diversity which, without belying the underlying unity of the many individual styles 'makes it a microcosm of black African art' is yet another of the distinguishing qualities of Nigerian art.'[5]

[5]Senghor, Leopold Sedar, op cit.

This powerful range of new influences rapidly found expression in his work, and his wooden panel reliefs reflect an abundance of different styles struggling to find expression. Later pieces such as the 'Cloth Market Series,' renderings in wood of the exciting visual juxtapositions of colourful cloths found in the market places or 'Kenté-Akwete Synthesis' show how distinctive elements of textile design from very different sources can be mixed in a single work to create bold visual disjunctions that the piece itself must actively struggle to resolve and hold in a formal balance. Such work, where the multiplicity of varied styles vying for the eye's attention is ultimately subsumed to an articulate controlling design, could almost be regarded as emblematic representations of 'natural synthesis' achieved.

To his previous fondness for Ghanaian Ewe and Asante textile designs Anatsui discovered in Nigeria new possibilities afforded by the Igbo *uli* and Efik *nsibidi* systems of representation, the whole contributing to an ever more powerful urge on his part to explore the ideograms and pictographic scripts of other African written languages. Such research into these areas led to his becoming something of a polyglot of visual sign languages, studying the Nigerian Yoruba scripts, the Bolange scripts of East Africa, the Mande script from Cameroon and numerous others.[6]

[6]'Sankofa: Go Back an' Pick.' op cit.

Perhaps, here, in the wealth of co-existing graphic styles competing against, borrowing from and interacting with each other to create new forms enriched with hybrid vigour, lies the source of the raw energy and resilience that Okeke ascribed to traditional Nigerian art. To those artists living within such a multi-cultural melting-pot of styles, ideas and forms, once comfortable and conversant with the flourishing diversity, the transition to modern western modes is no more complicated than the learning of yet another 'strategy.' Anatsui and Okeke both, however, would stress that this facility to move easily between such different worlds is predicated upon having first absorbed one's local language and having a firm understanding of one's own roots and origins. 'Unless a culture has strength, it cannot contribute to a universal dispensation, and that perhaps, is why it is dangerous for an artist to throw away his cultural heirloom and superficially take on an alien one. Any such artist has no confidence in his own work and his work is unlikely to be viable or virile, and thus irrelevant. It is only when one proceeds from a position of clear knowledge and definition of oneself that one stands a bright chance of contributing to whatever culture formation eventually emerges.'[7]

[7]'Sankofa: Go Back an' Pick.' op cit.

El Anatsui and the Transvangarde

I am suggesting here that the kind of multi-cultural environment that the *transvangarde* requires to flourish today is one for which many previous models have existed in different places and at different times. I am further suggesting that artists, such as Okeke and Anatsui, be seen as types of the *transvangarde* artist. They understood perfectly how simply appropriating the cast-off forms of other artists or cultures produces nothing of lasting merit, and betrays ones art to irrelevance in the process. They realised that only by sustained self-scrutiny could they trace their way back to construct an artistic identity that would reflect the value of their proper cultures, but that such 'clear knowledge and definition of oneself,' once discovered, would be sufficiently resilient to allow adaptation and transformation into other modes and styles without sacrificing anything essential in the process. Both artists were rigorous enough in their studies to 'go back and pick up' what was inherently valuable in their root traditions before immersing themselves in the 'strategies' of other neighbouring cultures. By absorbing the diverse grammars of other African styles they could exploit both similarities and differences, which added to their understanding of their own cultures even as it enabled them to see further beyond them. In an interview with Chika Okeke, Anatsui refers to how easy he found it to browse amongst these other styles springing from a common source, what he aptly terms a 'continental culture.' 'You see the cultures of Africa, no matter how diverse seem to have a common binding factor. So if I am taking from another African culture apart from mine, I am still very much within my culture, my continental culture.'[8] This is somewhat analogous, perhaps, to the way that learning Greek, Latin and, say German allows one to understand one's own English better, even as it enables one to perceive things that cannot be said in that language, for these languages too, all share a 'continental culture.' Anatsui's consequent ability to return to the western models he'd earlier rejected, and produce highly articulate works capable of being read by a contemporary western audience, yet remaining African to the core, marks the full attainment of Okeke's ideal of a 'natural synthesis.' It also, when the work shifts effortlessly between African and western aesthetic sensibilities, mastering both but belonging to neither one exclusively, makes an appropriate example of the *transvangarde.*

One piece that illustrates beautifully this manner in which El Anatsui grounds his work in an African context, investing it with concerns specific to that experience, without rendering it impermeable to other readings, is *Adinsibuli Stood Tall* (colour plate, p37). This is one of numerous pieces made in recent years from old mortars that were originally used for the extraction of palm-oil from the palm-fruit. The taking of an old, hollowed-out tree-trunk that has been so battered over the years as to become useless as a containing vessel and has therefore been discarded, and the transformation of this worthless and rejected object into art gives an insight into Anatsui's ways of working. There is an implicit recognition, here, that the surface value of an object may not be a true index of its worth, but depends on the viewer and what he or she can invest in that object. Found objects, for example, even those that no longer have any functional value, may still tell stories, and even reveal whole histories. Indeed it is the very facts of the mortar's having been pounded to the point of breaking, of its having outlived its 'utility' and been discarded, that enrich it with a specific 'history' and endow it with a power and presence of its own. Having refashioned the mortar by the simple means of upending it and adding a piece broken from another mortar to represent a head,

[8] 'Slashing wood, eroding Culture: Conversation with El Anatsui,' by Chika Okeke, *NKA: Journal of Contemporary African Art*, Fall/Winter 1994, p35.

Anatsui needed only to add small decorative touches to its surface to flesh out the mythic presence the historic mortar now acquires.

The figure is detectably that of a woman, standing with a gently swaying motion of her hips. Metal rings decorate her neck, and a few thinly beaten metal shapes, ornament her brow and the angle where her arm joins her body. The inner surface is engraved with a series of abstract coloured shapes, signs and symbols seemingly without order, some of which pick out and highlight the surface crevices of the weathered wood. No more is needed than to add touches of bright red lacquer to her fingernails, and 'Adinsibuli' stands before us complete, swaying with an arrested motion of mute eloquence. As we look closely at the coloured shapes that decorate the wooden surface we are aware that the different forms have different origins. The long cursive lines decorating her body are *uli* figures, recalling patterns the Igbo women would use to decorate themselves, others are *nsibidi* motifs, secret signs replete with hidden meanings used by a non-Igbo people, and still others, the repeating circular patterns below her bosom, recall the *adinkra* textile patterns of Asante cloth. These could all be seen simply as patterns decorating Adinsibuli's clothes, but their presence, engraved on the inner surface, suggests a deeper meaning. What is certainly important is the *combination* of motifs, which coming from different ethnic origins are intermingled in a seemingly random way. That this mixture itself is central to the meaning of the work is confirmed by her name, which like the piece, a composite figure made up of disparate parts, is a compound name derived from the first two syllables of the three source words **Adi**nkra, **Nsi***b*idi and **Uli** — *Adinsibuli.* The overall thrust of the piece therefore speaks of the manner in which individuals such as Adinsibuli (who combines different cultures) and cultures (that are combinations of different individuals such as Adinsibuli) are both creatures constituted of heterogeneous parts. The final clue, presented in the title, is perhaps the message that this woman, representative of many generations of nameless women engaged in the repetitive process of extracting oil, should stand tall, proudly confident in the possession of a personal complex of inherited histories and cultures. Adinsibuli becomes an actor who, in this drama, stands proudly forward and speaks her name, thereby expressing that 'clear knowledge and definition of herself' — her true identity, based on the enriching combination of a plurality of cultures. The discarded mortar has been redeemed and transformed by Anatsui into an eloquent subject for contemplation — the *object* is made *art.*

In a later essay in this book, the Japanese author, Yukiya Kawaguchi, records in fine detail the sequence of feelings through which he came to understand another installation, *On Their Fateful Journey Nowhere (colour plate, pp2-3)*. To Mr. Kawaguchi, the meaning of the piece was finally revealed when he heard it 'speak' directly to him, and he was reminded of the powerful urgency of a speech made by the chorus in a Greek drama. Adinsibuli, too is an actor, and to record my own feelings before her, I have to refer to the Japanese Noh drama. To take a representative example of this highly stylised form: a traveller on a lonely beach feels drawn towards a wind-blasted pine-tree; mesmerised by some strange quality of the tree he becomes aware of the arrival of a woman who, as he questions her, reveals that her name is 'pine,' and that she, who is now the spirit of the tree, had once been human; she recounts the story of an intense passion that binds her to the place, and disappears, leaving the traveller alone to 'pine' and muse upon her Fate.

Were Adinsibuli to speak, I know she would not use the eerie sing-song language of the Noh stage. Yet I am equally certain that the story she would 'tell' would be of a similar intensity and passion to the haunting tale of the Japanese spirit-lady. Adinsibuli also is bewitching and casts a spell. Something in the wood of this mortar mesmerises, and there is more that would speak also, locked into the coded signs that cover her body. If we listen she might tell stories of the things the women talked about as they pounded the palm-fruit together, might describe the changes occurring in the village that the mortar experienced and remembers from when she too had a position in the social life of the place. The more we know how to ask questions of her, the more she might reveal, but until we are mesmerised and ask — she remains a blasted tree-trunk, an old upended mortar.

What fascinates me here is that before one installation of old African wood, a Japanese man should experience an intense epiphany worthy of the Greek drama, and before another arrangement of old African wood an Englishman should be reminded of the Japanese drama, and both should be led by such circuitous routes to contemplate African experience. Something strange is happening here, though I cannot describe it better than by saying that what is common in each case is the intensity of the emotion evoked. I only know that the recognition of that strange something is an index of the quality of the art by which I am entranced. There is a something in *Adinsibuli Stood Tall* and *On Their Fateful Journey Nowhere* that escapes the boundary definitions of 'modern Ghanaian art' or 'contemporary Nigerian art,' or the 'Nsukka School' or any such label. Although the term is yet to be fully explored, it entails no specific dogma besides the insistence upon those qualities in art as produce such shifts into timeless reverie and the search for those artists who have escaped the gravity-wells of culture to create it — that is what I mean by *Transvangarde.*

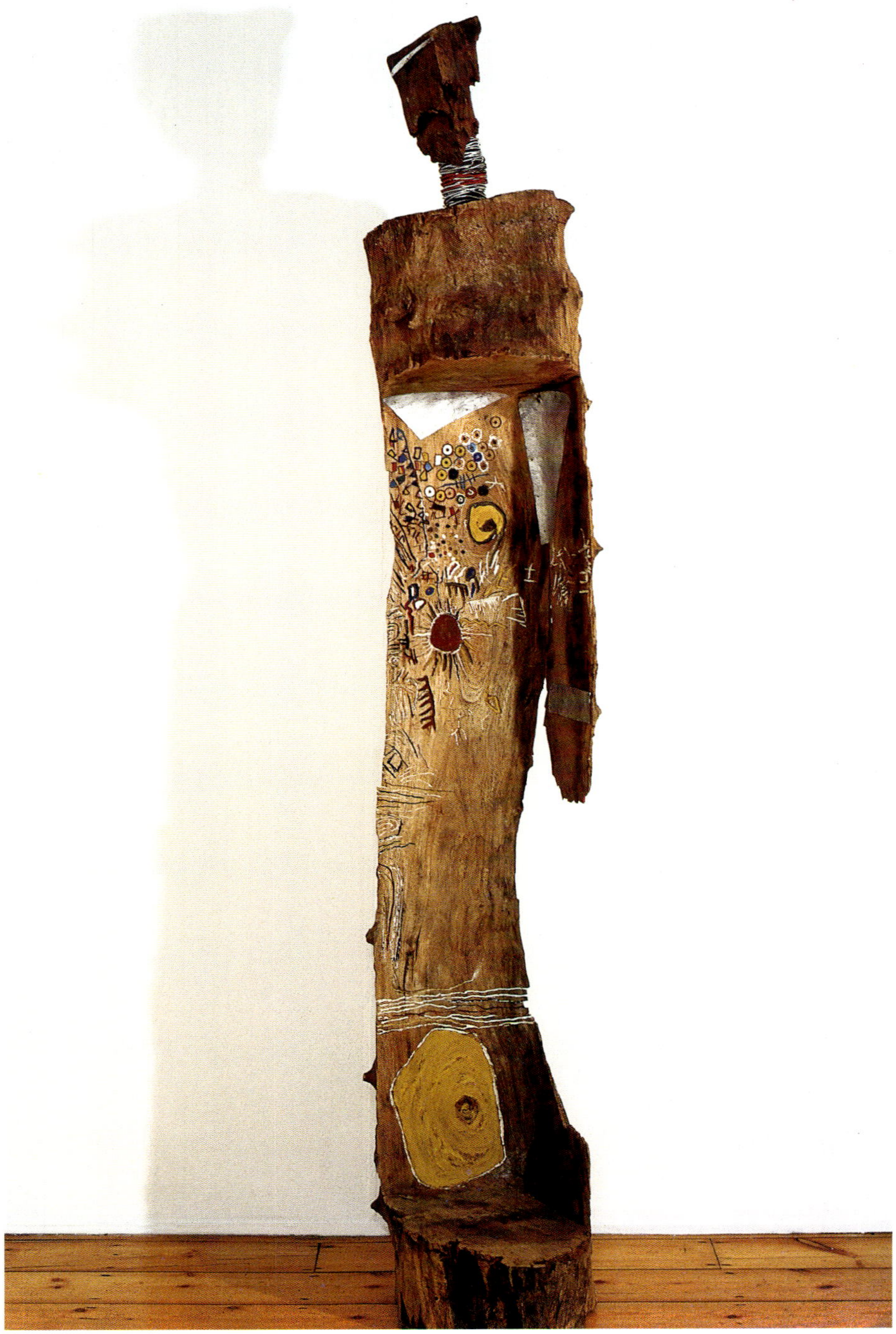

Adinsibuli Stood Tall, 1995

installation, iroko
& tempera
height 239cm, width
40cm, depth 37cm

Photo: Andy Keate

Akua's Surviving Children, 1996

installation, found wood & metal
height 165cm, width & depth variable

Photo: Andy Keate

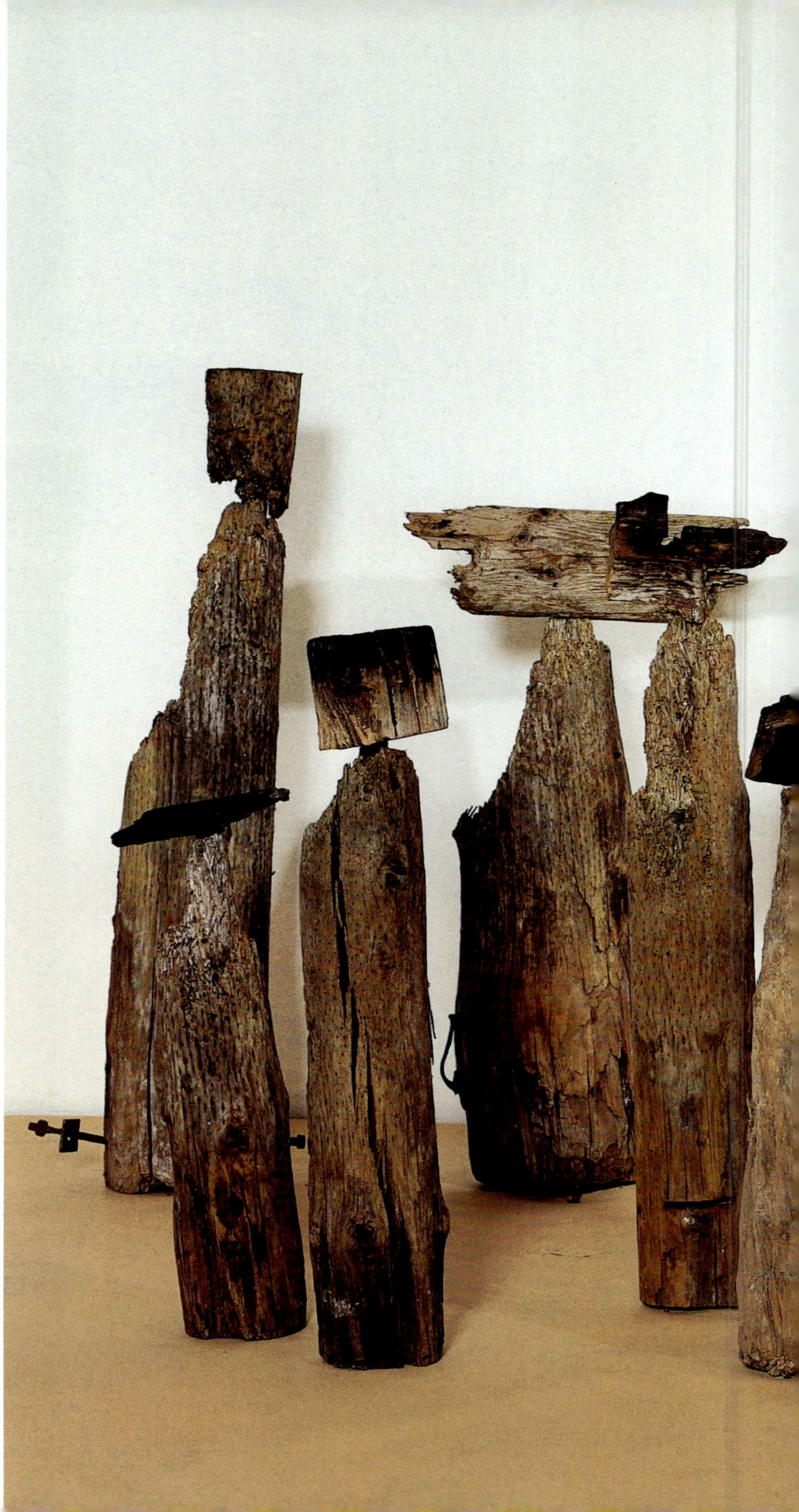

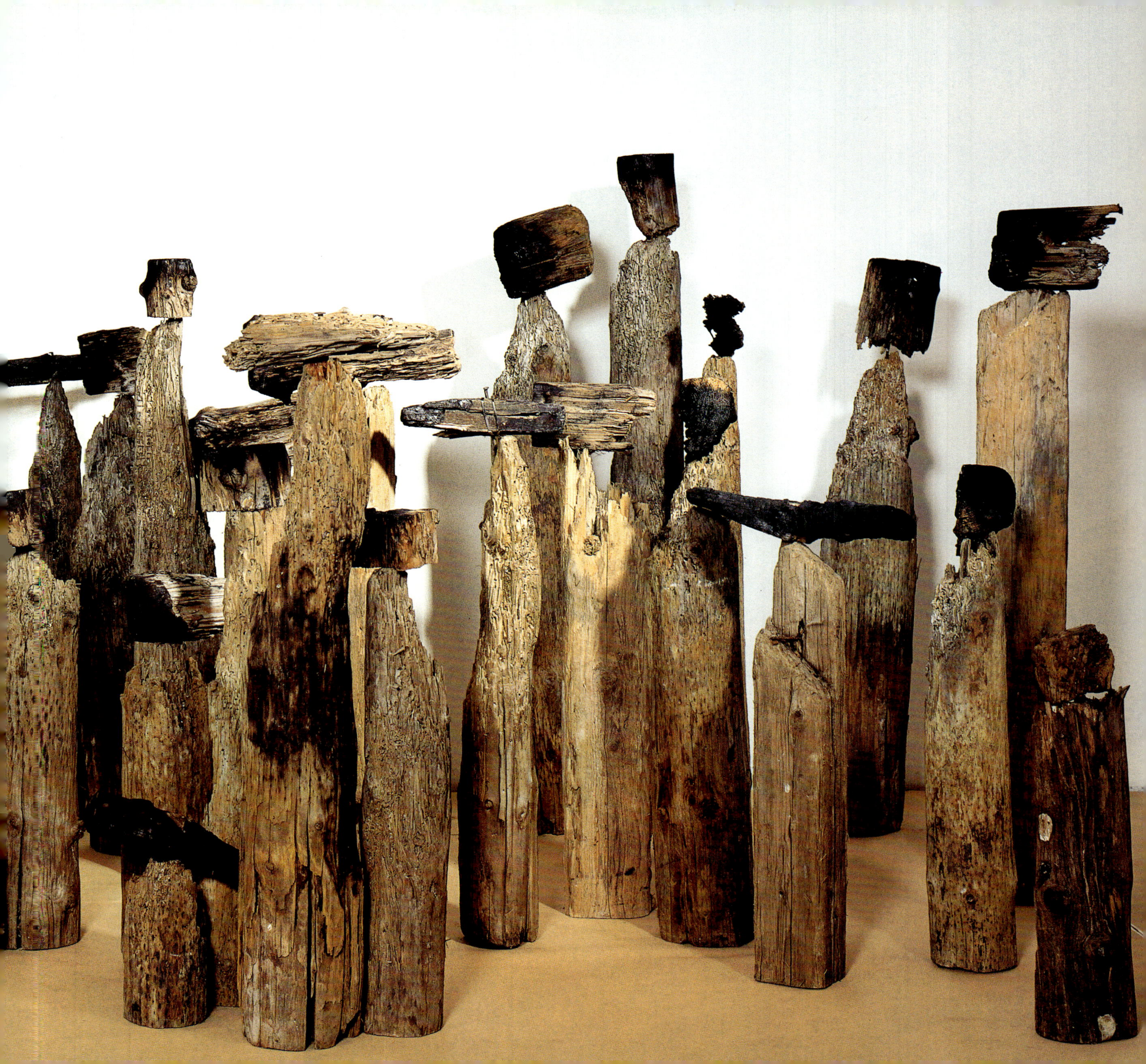

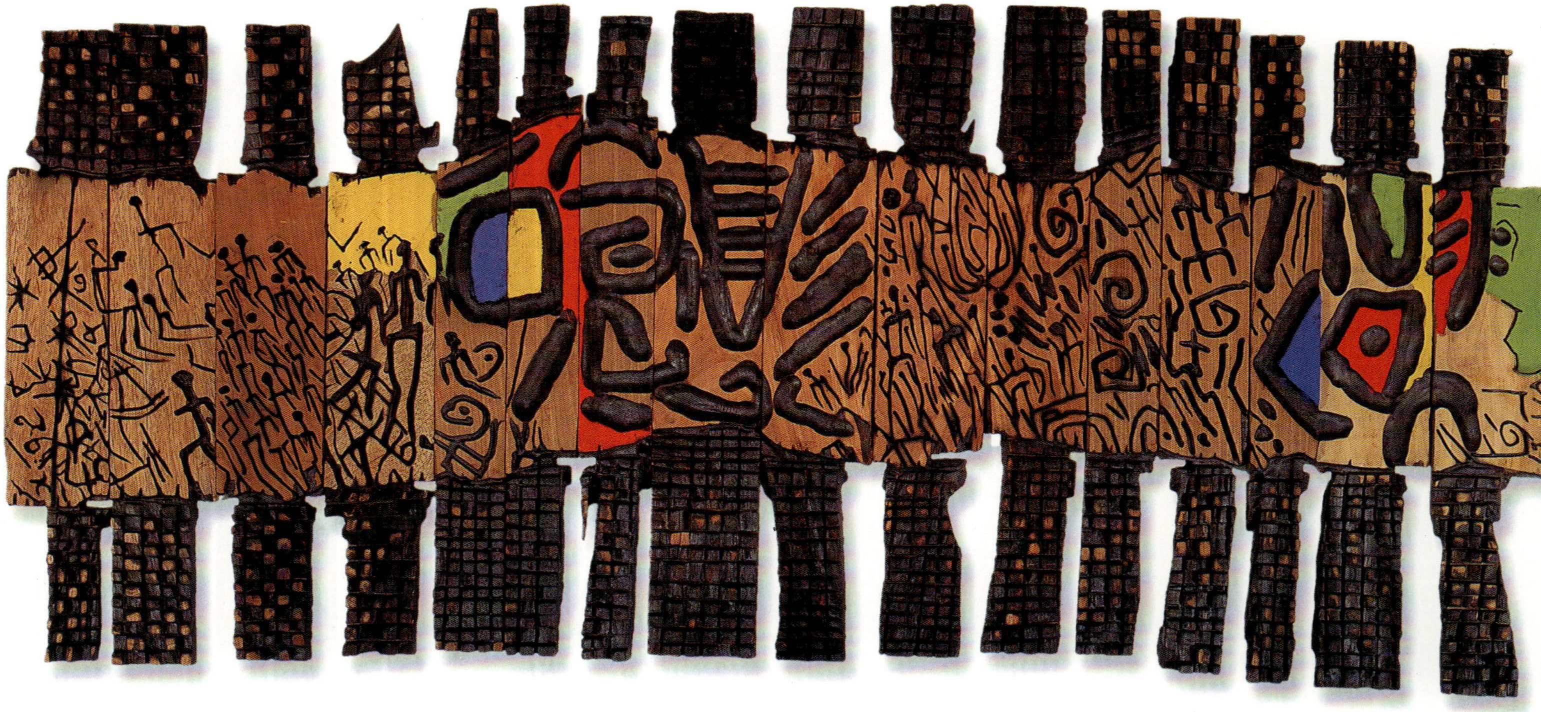

Unfolding the Scroll of History II, 1994

wood relief, oke-ofo, oyili-oji, akparata, okpo-ocha woods & tempera
height 61cm, width 141cm, depth 2.5cm

Photo: Andy Keate

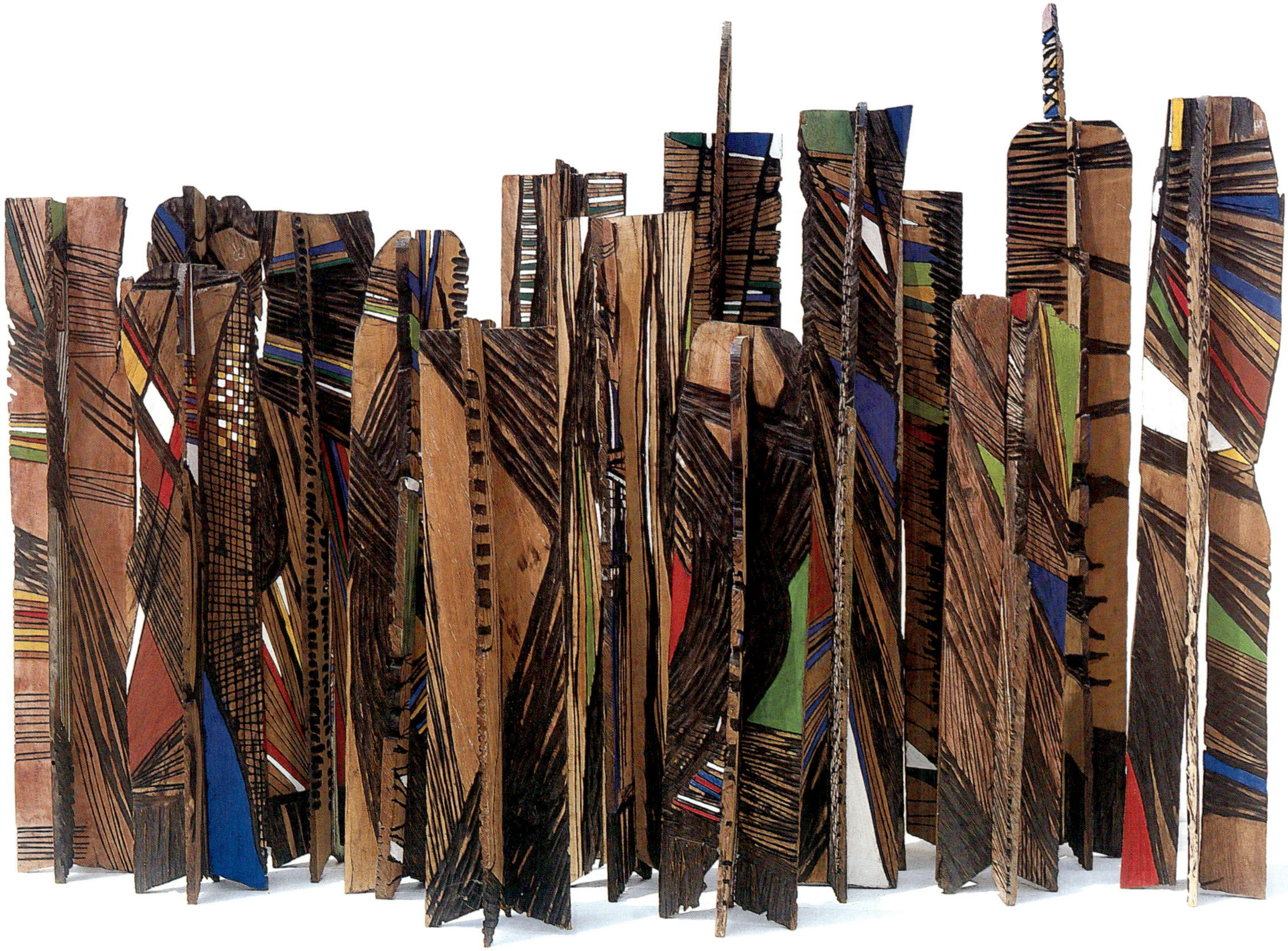

Africa - Internal Rhythms II, 1995

installation, iroko, oke-ofo & tempera
height 211cm, width & depth variable
Collection Hans-J Bogatzke

Photo: C O Amuzie

Earth-Moon Connexions, 1993

wood relief, okpo-ocha, oyili-oji & tempera height 90cm, width 84.4cm, depth 2.5cm

Collection of the National Museum of African Art, Smithsonian Institution, Washington DC, USA.

Photo: Franko Khoury

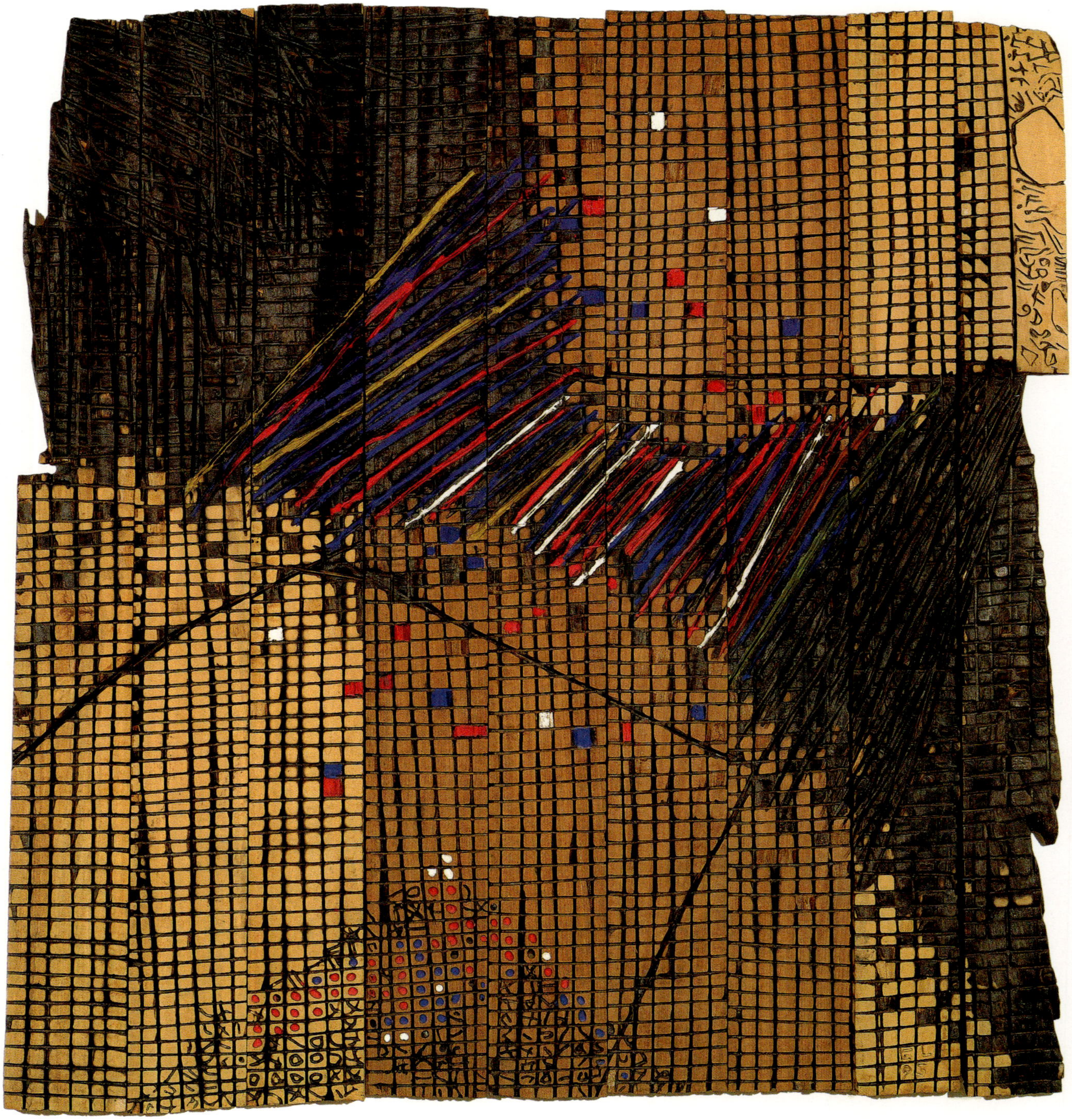

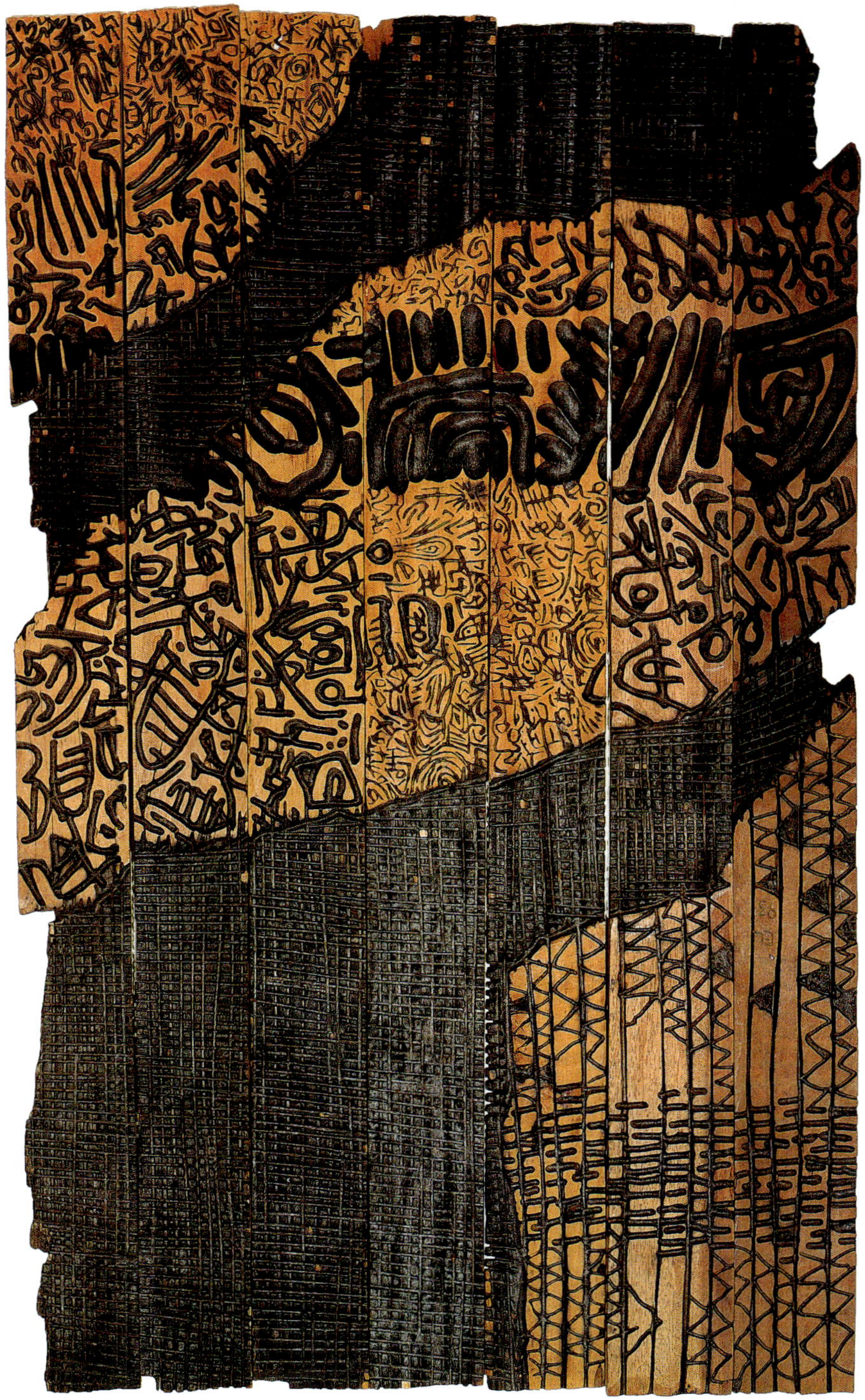

Patches of History III, 1993

wood relief, oyili-oji, opepe
& akparata woods
height 140cm, width 69cm,
depth 2.5cm

Photo: Franko Khoury

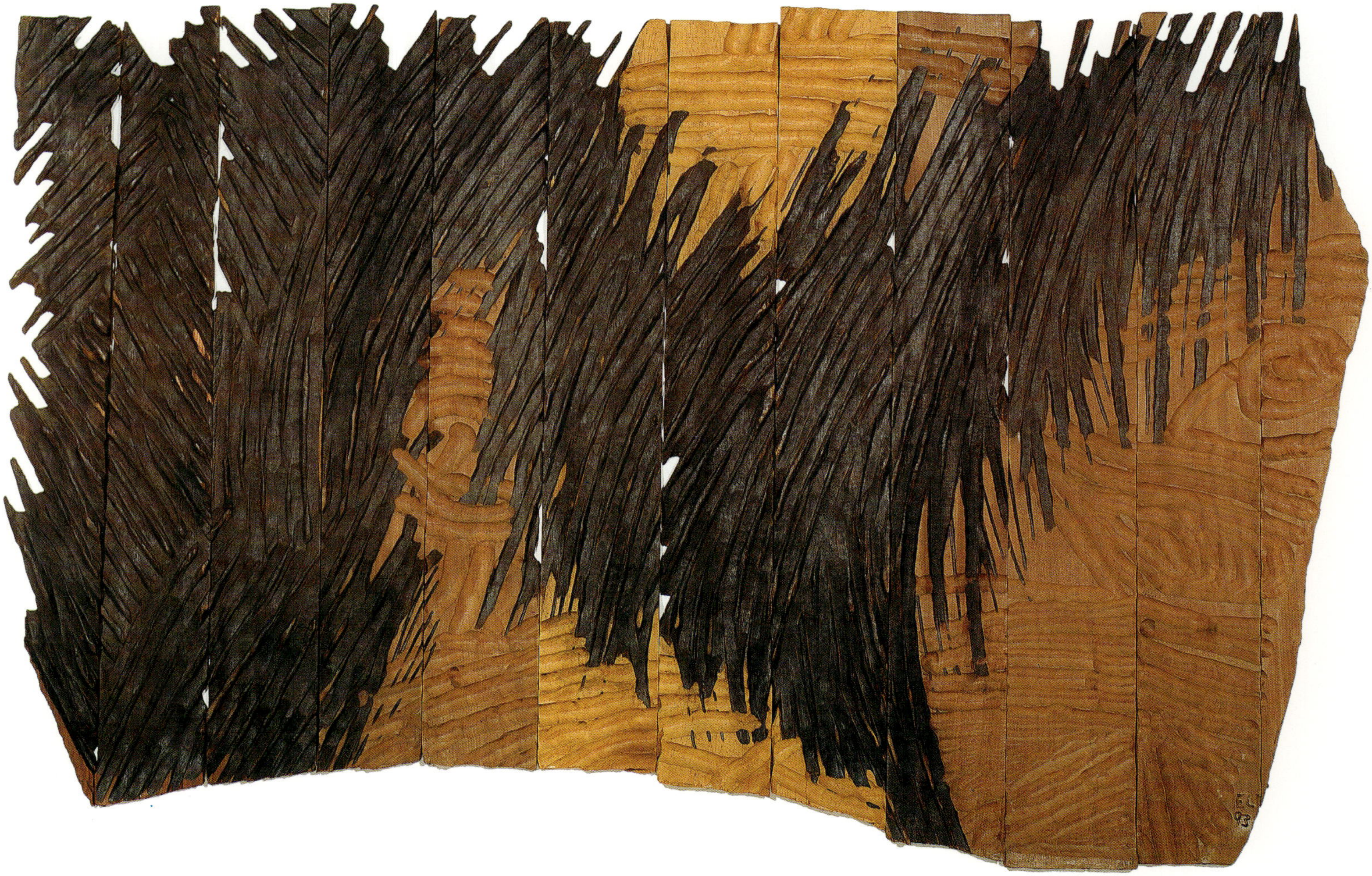

Undercurrents, 1993

wood relief, opepe, oyili-oji & camwood
height 76cm, width 118cm, depth 2.5cm

Photo: Franko Khoury

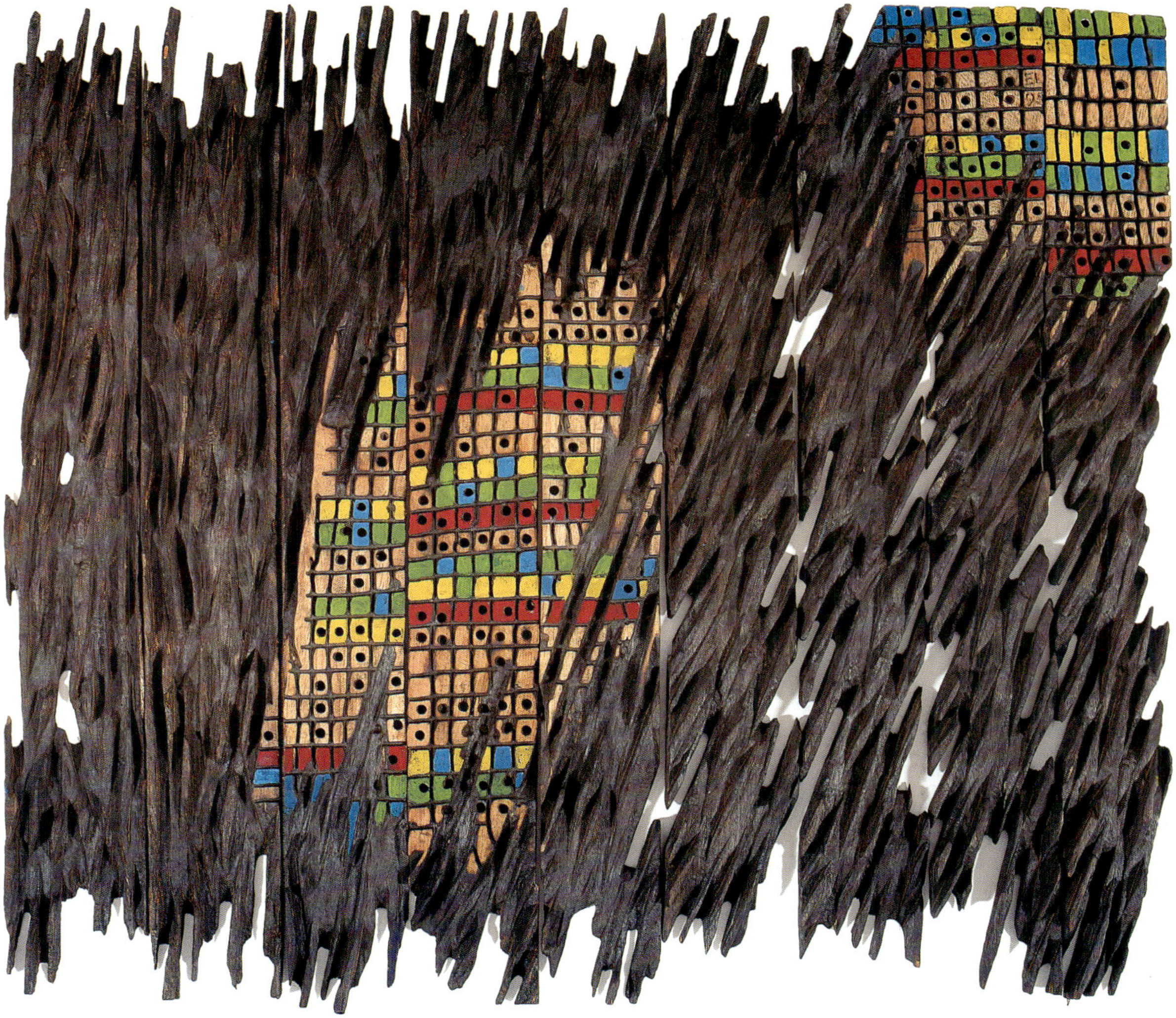

Remnant of Grandma's Cloth, 1995

wood relief, akparata, oke-ofo & tempera
height 80cm, width 92cm, depth 2.5cm

Photo: Andy Keate

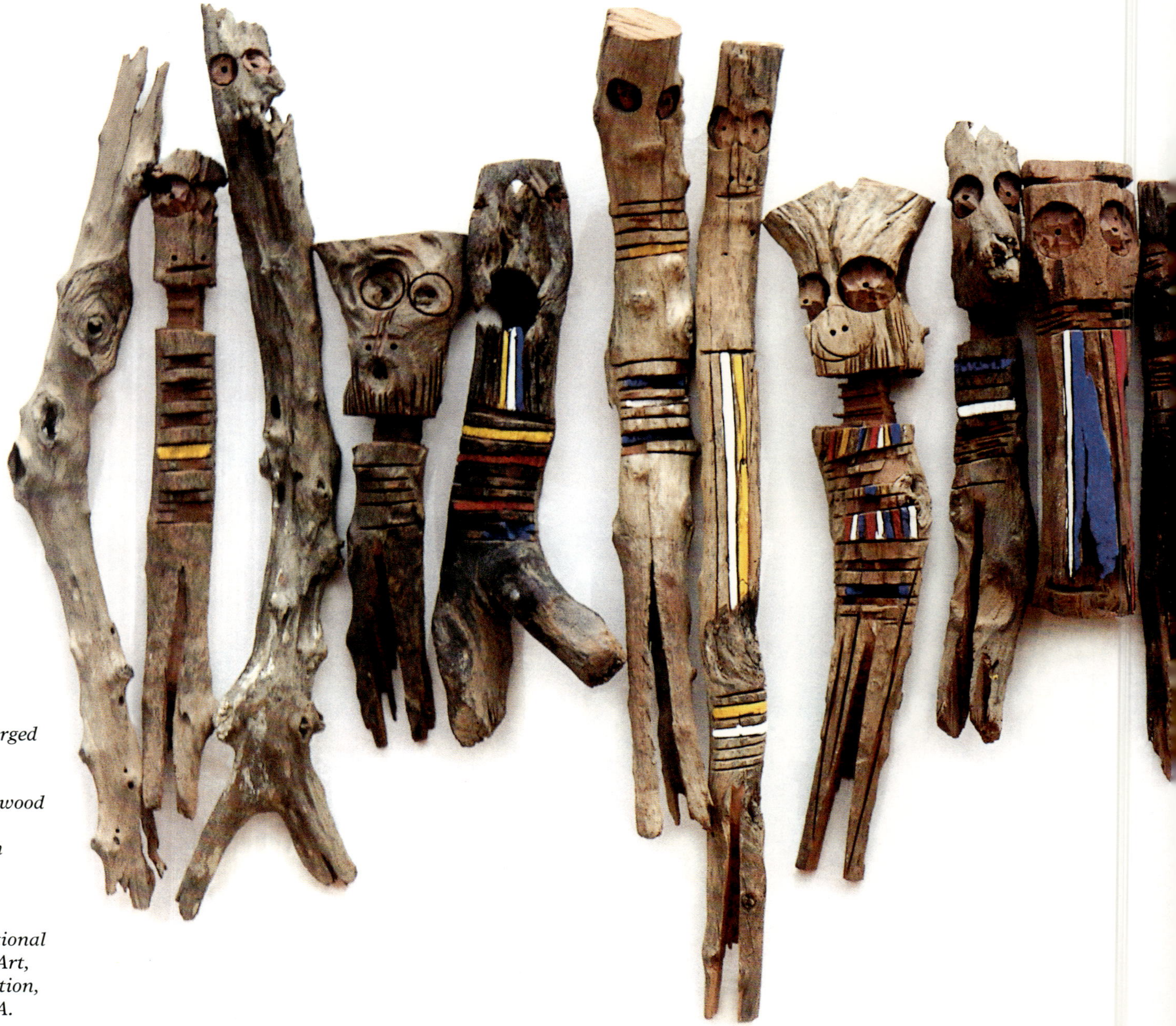

The Ancestors Converged Again, 1995

installation, okpeye wood & tempera
height 102cm, width 272cm, depth 15cm (variable)

Collection of the National Museum of African Art, Smithsonian Institution, Washington DC, USA.

Photo: C O Amuzie

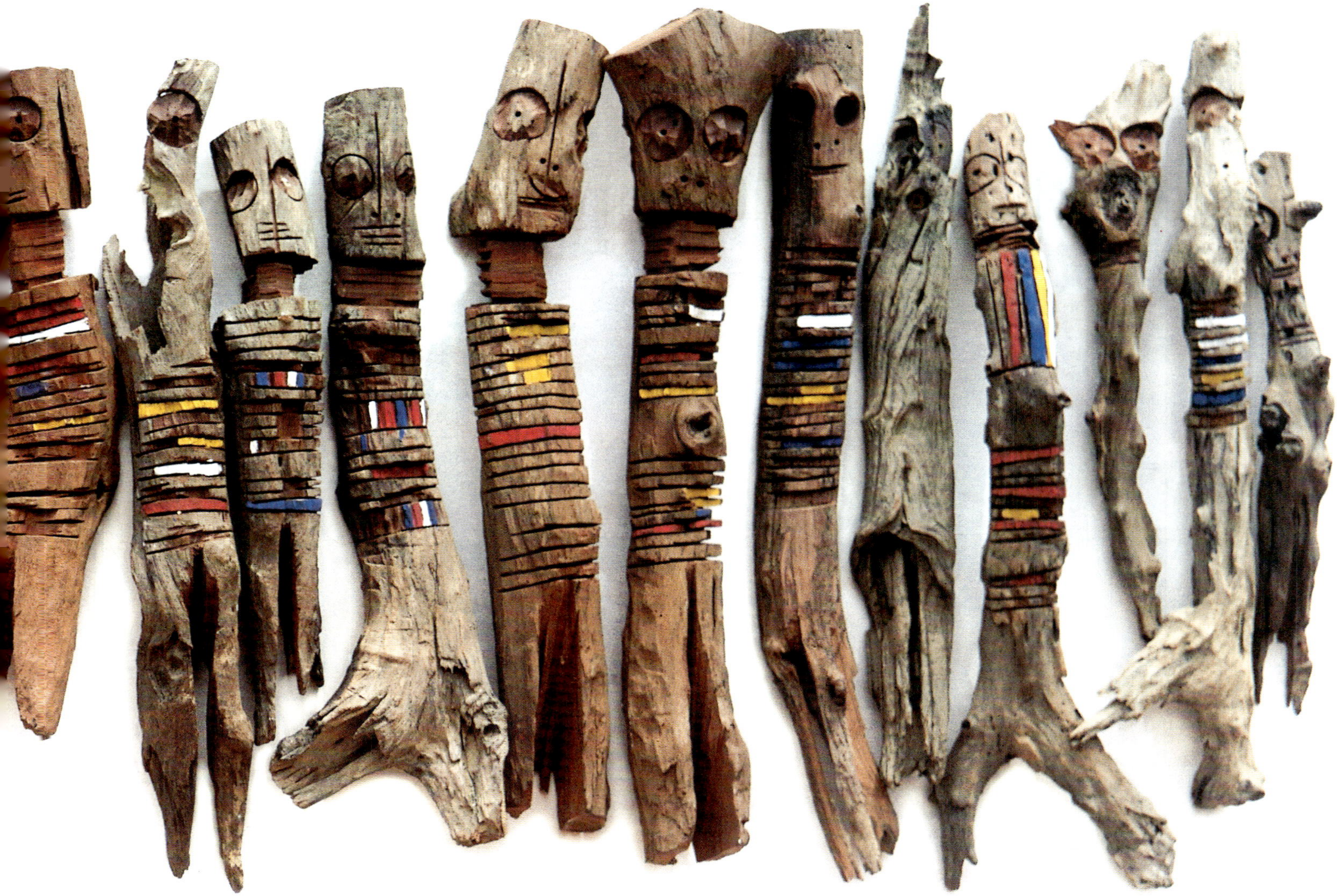

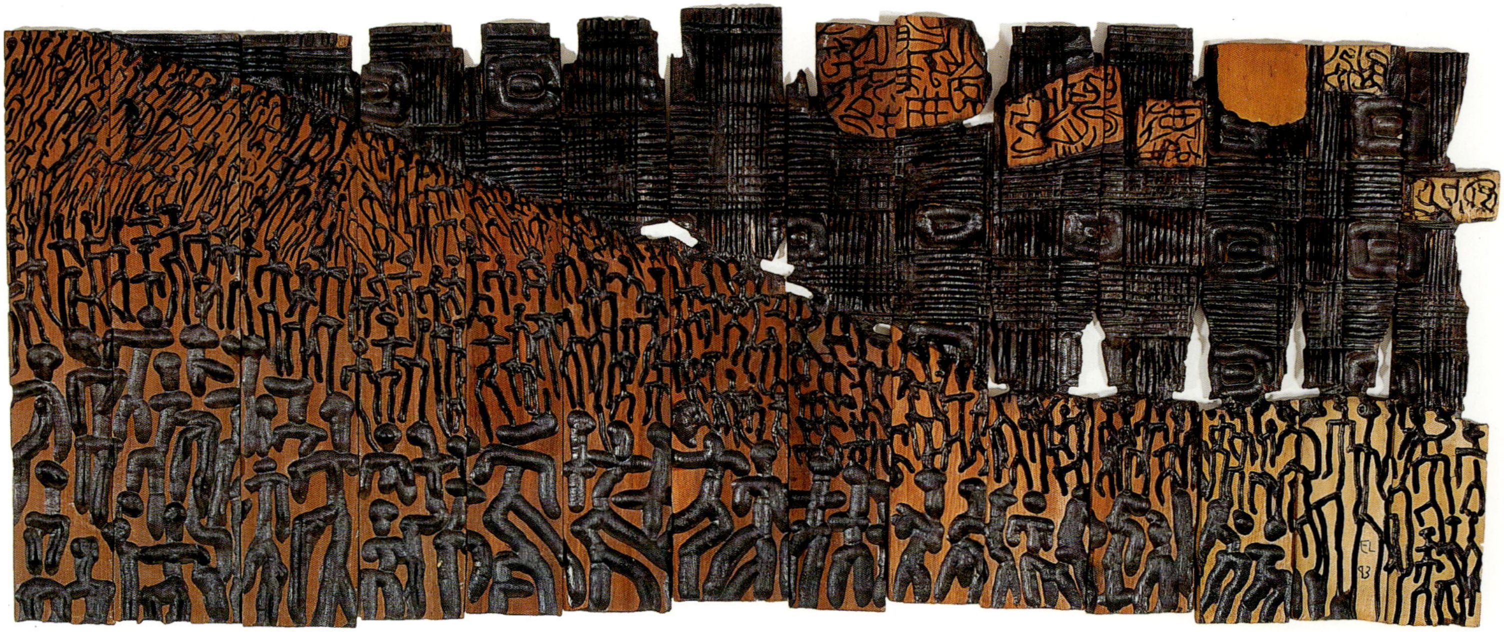

Mammoth Crowd Series I, 1993

wood relief, akparata, oke-ofo, oyili-oji & opepe woods
height 56cm, width 138cm, depth 2.5cm

Photo: Andy Keate

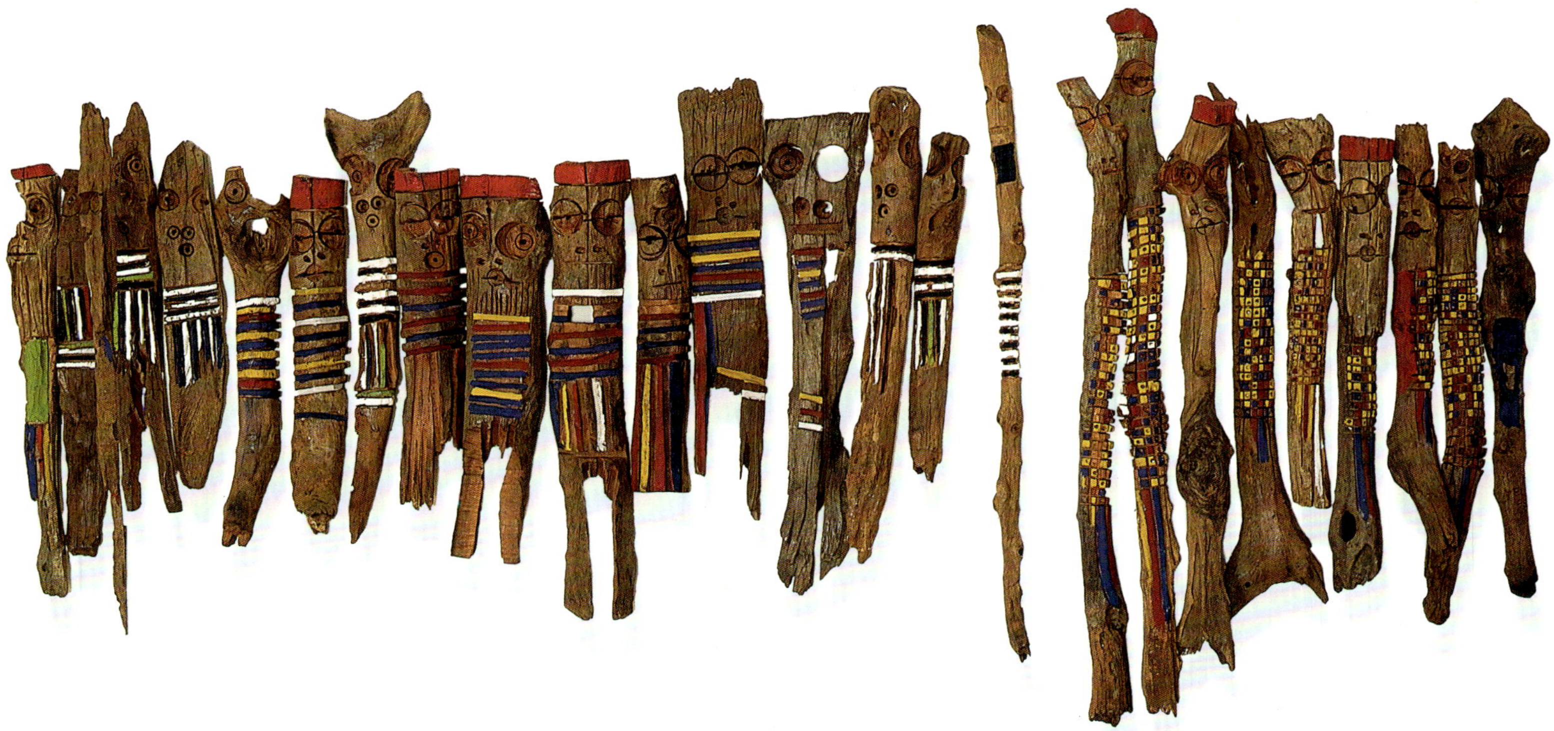

At the Ancestors' Conference II, 1995

installation, okpeye wood
height 100cm, width 220cm, depth 19cm (variable)

Collection of Hans J Bogatzke

Photo: Andy Keate

Tapper, 1995

mixed media, wood,
raffia, palm fibre & cloth
height 183 cm, width 60cm

Photo: El Anatsui

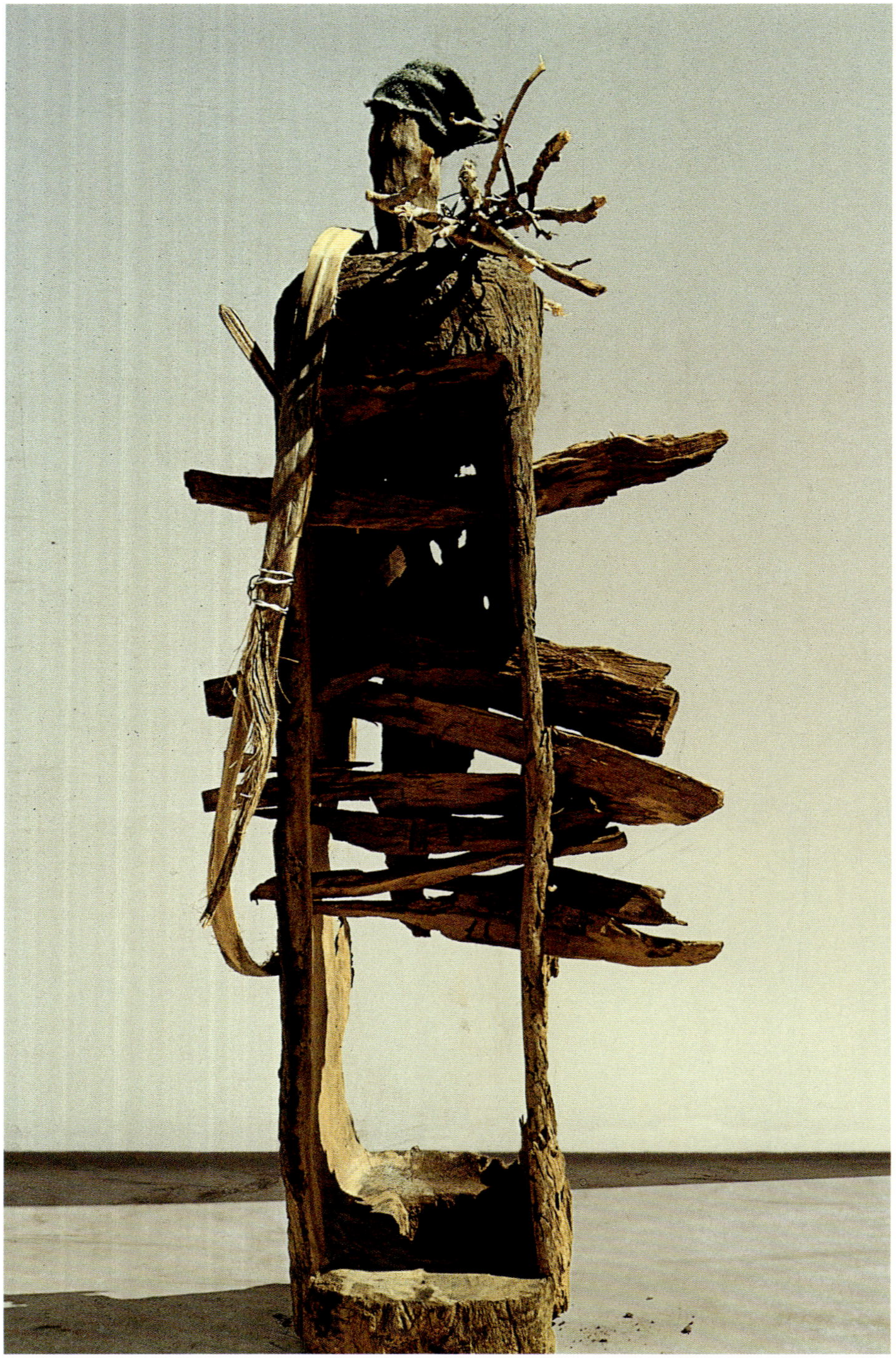

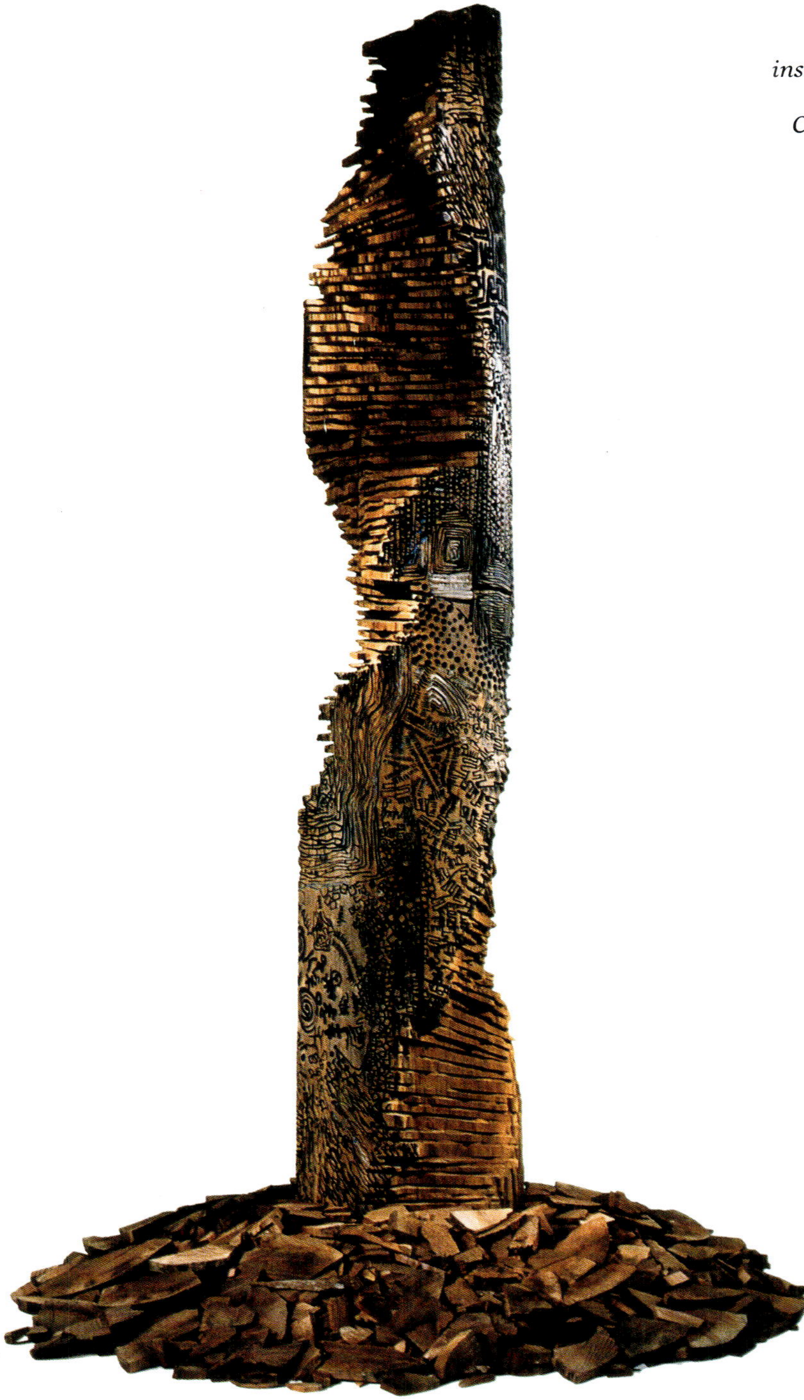

Erosion, 1992

installation, piqua-marfin & tempera
height 296cm
Collection of the National Museum
of African Art, Smithsonian
Institution, Washington DC, USA.

Photo: Franko Khoury

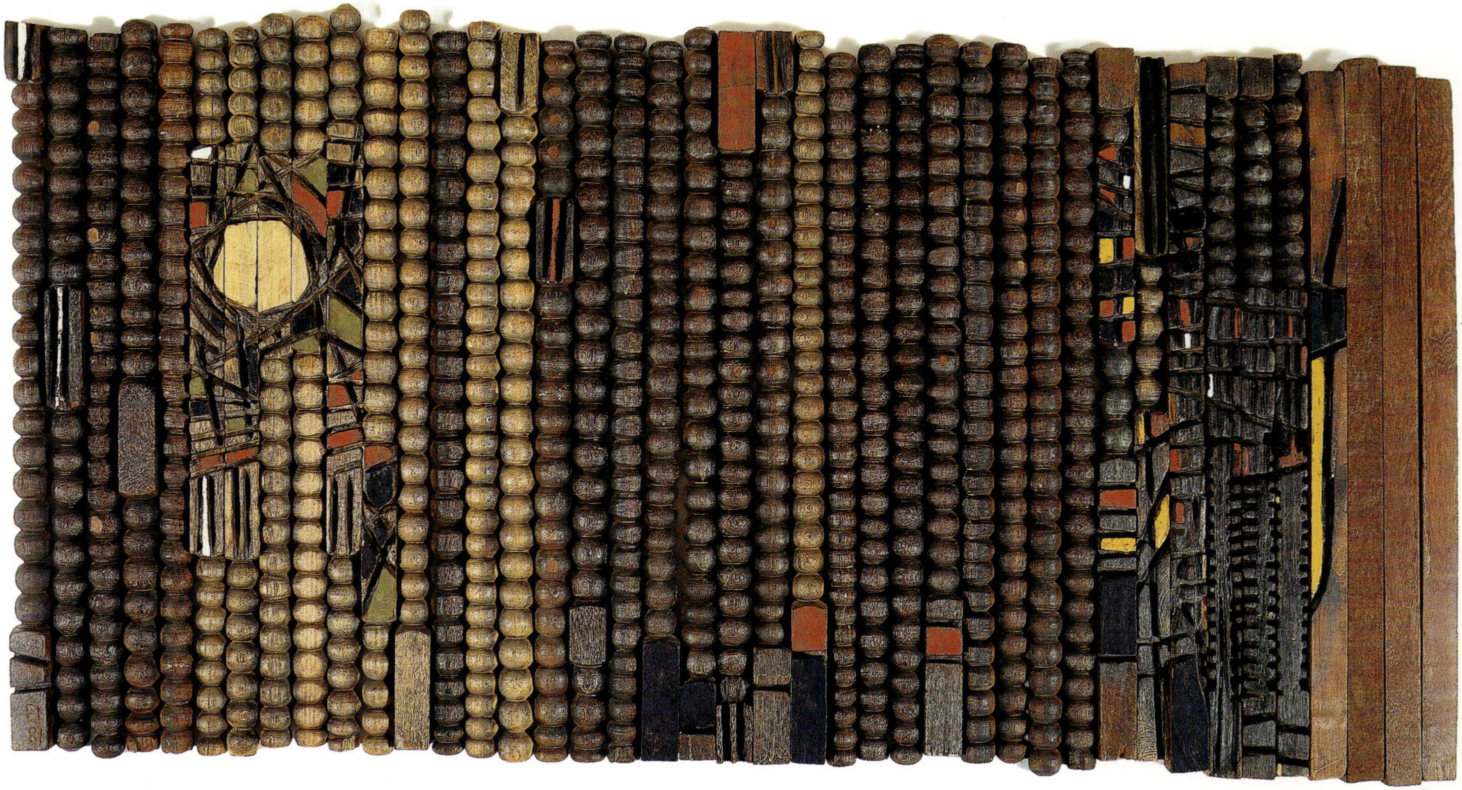

Moon and Stars, 1987

owen, oke-ofo, tempera & acrylic
height 97cm, width 184cm, depth 5cm

Photo: Andy Keate

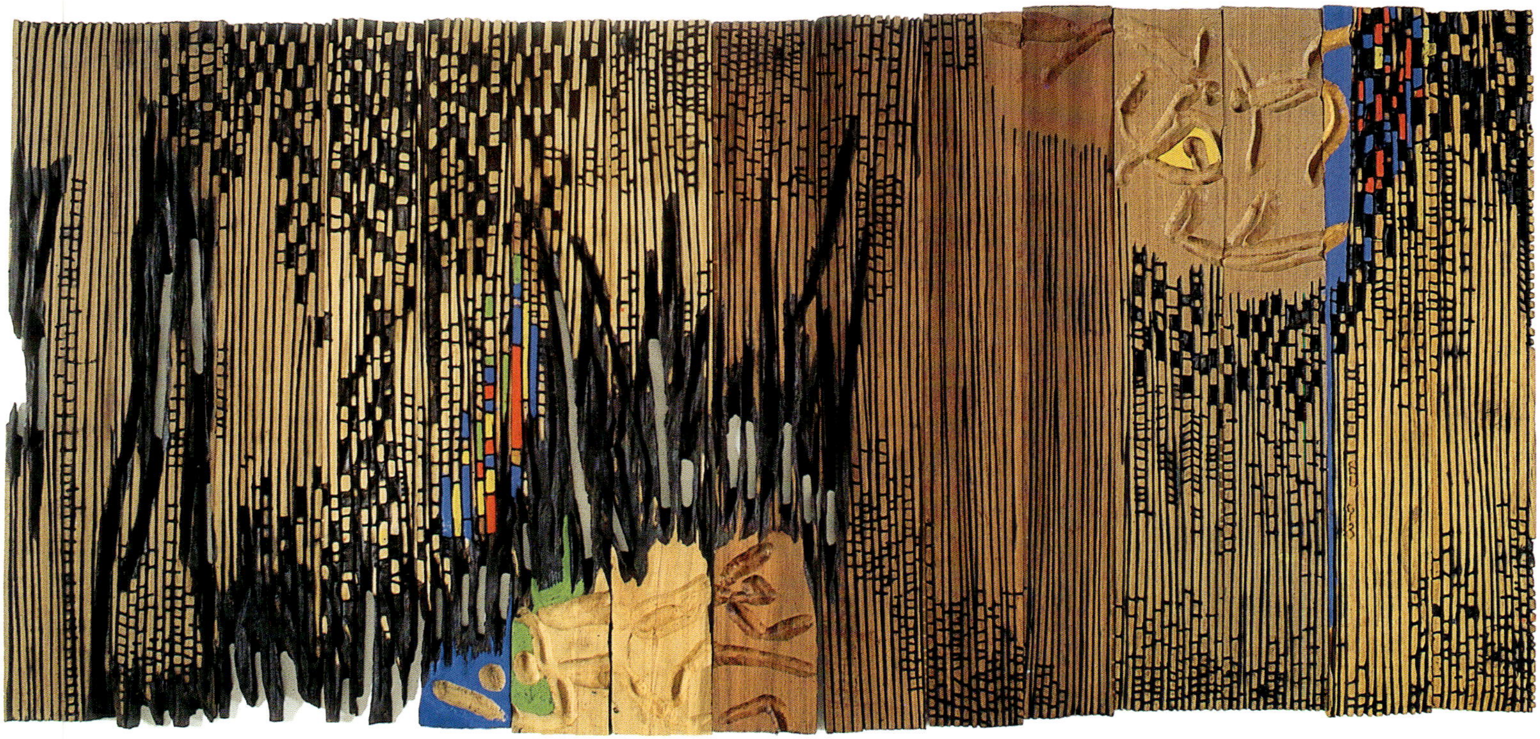

Ancient Cloth Series VIII, 1993

wood relief, okpo-ocha, oyili-oji,
opepe, oke-ofo & tempera
height 72cm, width 149cm, depth 2.5cm

Photo: Andy Keate

Wonder Masquerade II, 1990

standing figure, oak
height 159cm, width 20cm,
depth 14cm

Photo: Franko Khoury

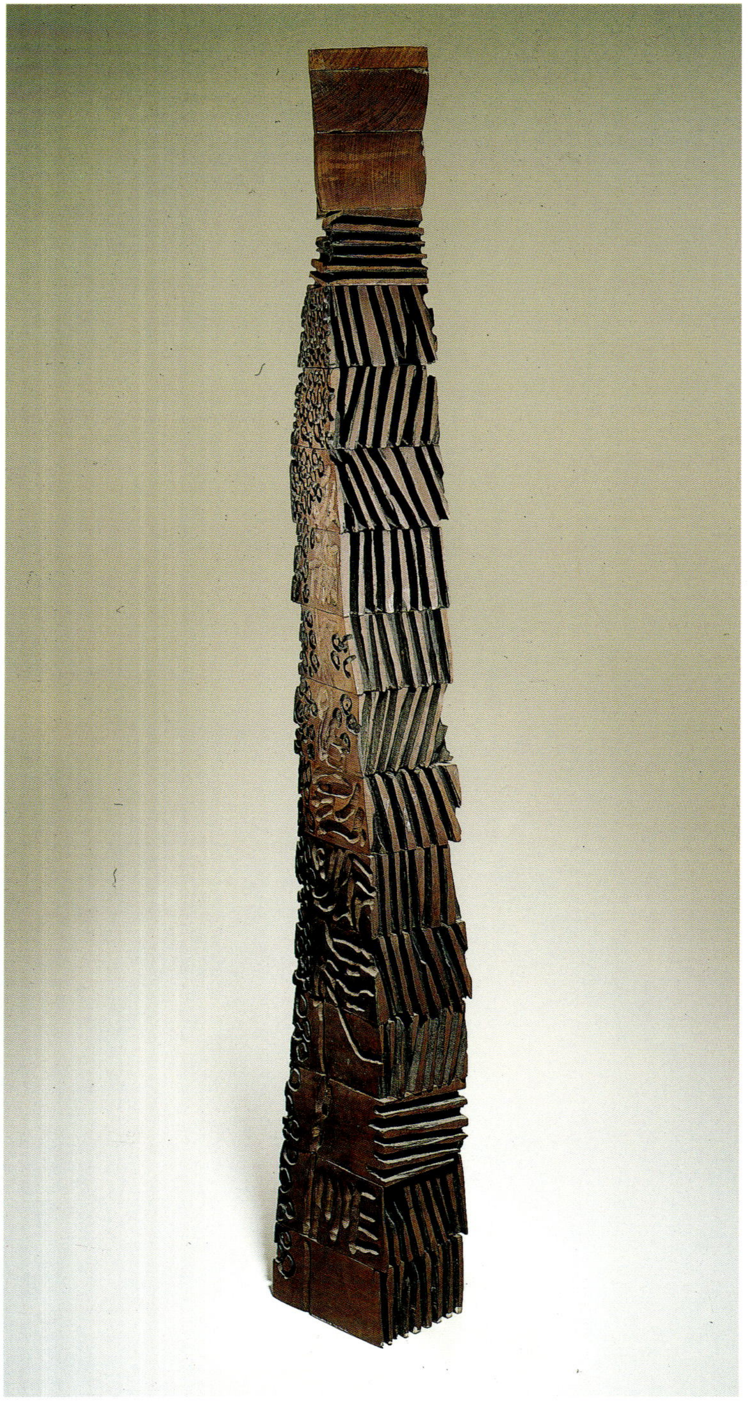

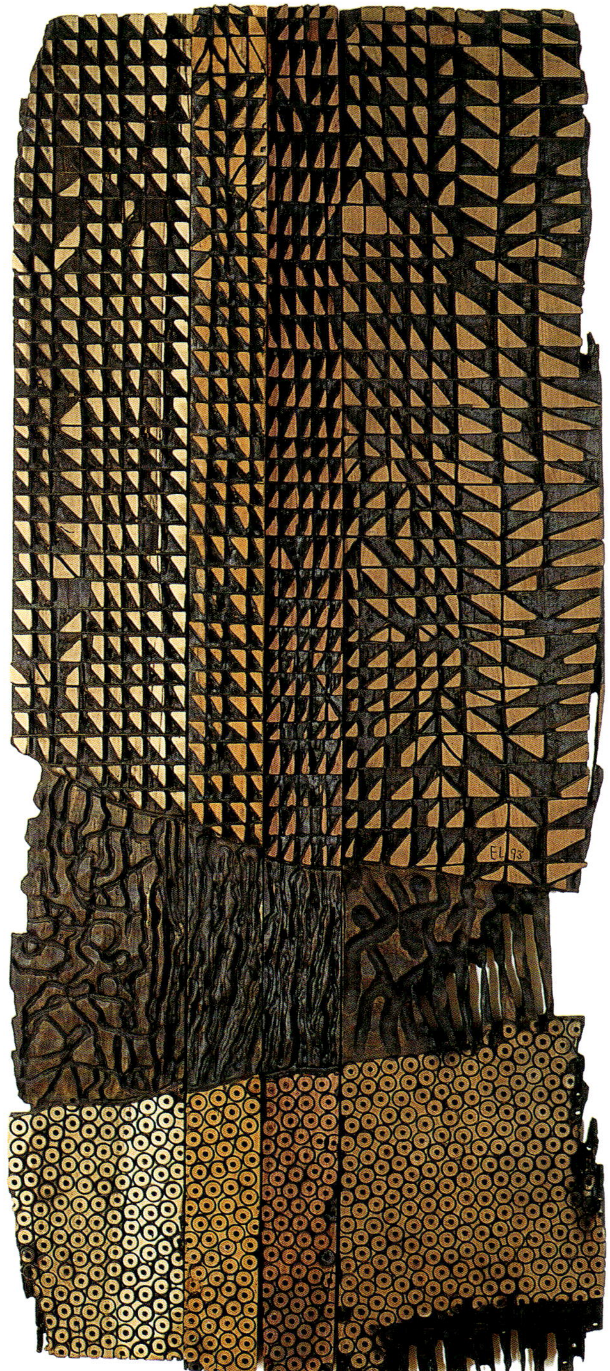

Leopard Cloth, 1993

wood relief, mansonia,
camwood, opepe & oyili-oji
height 162cm, width 69cm,
depth 3cm

Photo: Andy Keate

川口 幸也　　世田谷美術館 学芸員

エル・アナツイへの旅

春3月のニューヨークの天気は気まぐれだ。突然暖かい日がっやってきたかと思うと、そのすぐ次の日にはまた真冬に逆戻りする。エル・アナツイの作品を初めて目にしたのは、たしか1990年の3月、暖かった方の日のニューヨークでだった。ちょうどハーレム地区にあるスタジオ・ミュージアムで行われていた、「変貌する伝統」という、アフリカ現代美術の9人の作家にスポットを当てた展覧会に、出品作家として選ばれていたのだ。アフリカの現代美術を扱う展覧会というのは、このごろではさほど珍しくもないが、その当時では、かなり目新しい試みであった。

アナツイの作品はいかにもモダーンだ。「プリミティヴ」な作風をお目当てに会場にやってきたアフリカ美術のよき理解者たちは、まず彼の作品から挨拶がわりの軽いジャブを食らうことになる。チェーンソーで乱暴に切られた、何枚かのスキー板状の細長い板が十枚前後、ぴたっと縦に重なって作り上げる小さな平面。それぞれの板の長さは一様ではないから、全体しての形は、まるでジグソーパズルの破片のようにまちまちである。もっとも大きさは縦横1メートル以上もあり、はるかに大きいが。ところどころ灼きごてを当てられたのように黒く灼けた跡が残り、別のところには青や赤の絵の具で何かの記号が小さく描きこまれている。ソフトにまとめ上げられた、洒落た作品だ。

それからほぼ一年後、ちょうど世界が湾岸戦争直前で揺れていたころ、私は、ナイジェ

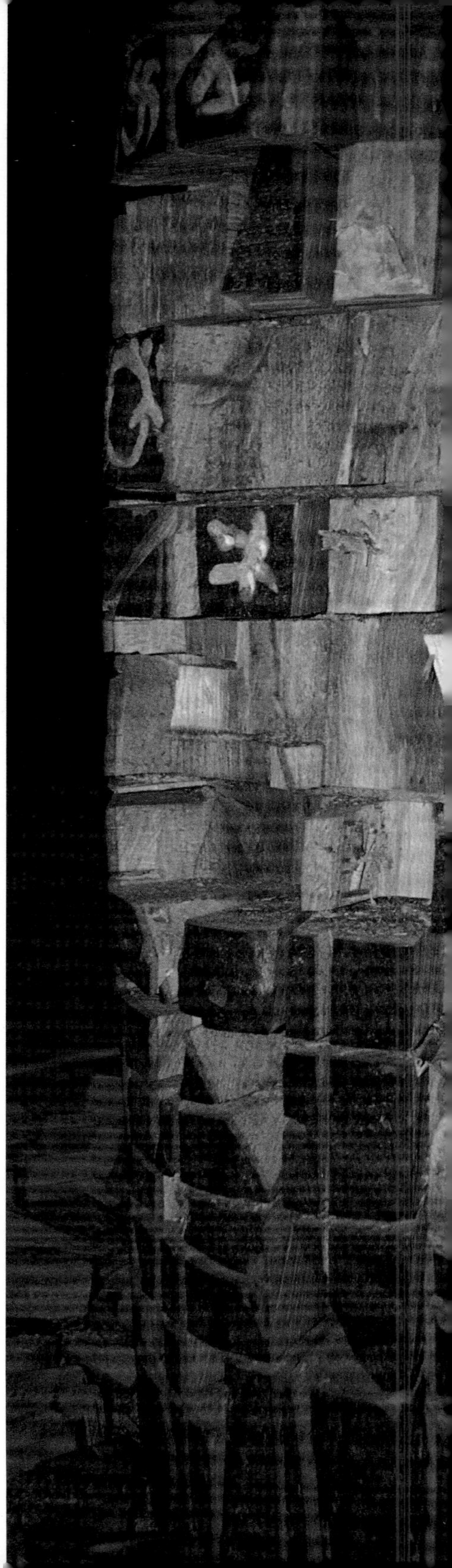

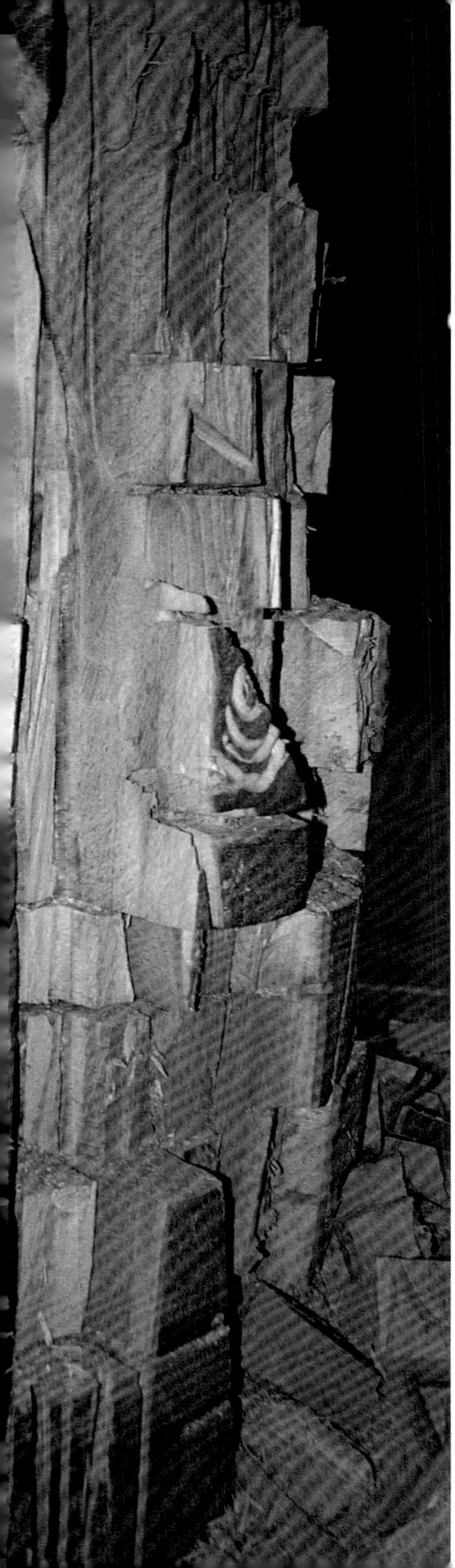

YUKIYA KAWAGUCHI

A Fateful Journey

NEW YORK in March: the weather is unpredictable. Just when you think it's turning unexpectedly warm, the following day drops you back into the depths of midwinter. It was on just such a warm New York day, back in March of 1990, that I first set eyes on the work of El Anatsui. He had been chosen as one of nine exhibiting artists in a show of contemporary African art entitled *A Changing Tradition* then showing at the Studio Museum in Harlem. Although nowadays exhibitions of contemporary African art are not that unusual, at the time they were sufficiently rare as to create quite an impression.

The work El Anatsui had on exhibition in Harlem was strikingly *modern*, and must have come as a mild shock to any lovers of African art who had gone along to the gallery expecting to see something more 'primitive.' He had taken roughly about nine or ten long, thin, wooden planks that had been scored with a chainsaw and hung them alongside each other to create a planar relief. Since the boards were of varying lengths and different sizes the overall effect was rather like that of a complex jigsaw-puzzle. These particular jigsaw-puzzles, however, were large, being more than a metre wide overall. There were patches on them where the wood had been scorched to a charcoal black and other places where the fine details of small symbols had

---

Yukiya Kawaguchi is the Chief Curator of the Setagaya Art Museum, Tokyo, a Research Associate of the National Museum of Ethnology, Osaka and a lecturer at Gakushuin and Rikyo (Saint Paul's) Universities, Tokyo. With exhibitions such as African Art Now *at The Japan Foundation (1993) and the successful touring exhibition* An Inside Story: African Art of Our Time *(1995) he has pioneered, almost single-handedly, the introduction of contemporary African art to Japanese museums and galleries. As the International Commissioner of* Dak'Art *(The 1996 Biennale of Dakar) he also co-ordinated the international symposium Representing 'Cultures' in Musuems: Cultural Exhibitions in the 21st Century (1997). He has recently been a consultant to the Kansai Museum of Ethnography, the British Museum and the Museum of Mankind, on a collaborative exhibition of African and Oceanic Art. An admirer of the work of El Anatsui, Yukiya Kawaguchi has been responsible for the acquisition of several important installations for the Setagaya Art Museum.*

リア東部にある、なだらかな高原に囲まれた小さな大学町ンスカで、実際に彼のアトリエを訪ねる機会を得た。大学からほんの少し車を走らせた所にある、彼のアトリエに足を踏み入れると、おが屑の香しい香りがぷーんと鼻をついてきた。真っ暗なアトリエの裸電球のスイッチをひねると、はたして足下の土の上には細かなおが屑が真っ白く降り積もっていた。そこで彼は、いくつもの作品を奥から取り出してきては、次から次へと見せてくれた。その時の作品は、大きく分けて二つの傾向に分類することができた。ひとつはニューヨークで見たのと同じように細長い板を縦に密着させて、ひとつの平面を構成するものであり、もうひとつはブロック状の木を高く積み上げて、人物を象ったものである。私は、彼の話をいろいろ聞きながら、だが、実際に作品を目の前にした印象を、明確な言葉に置き換えるができないもどかしさの中にいた。

その夜、私はンスカにある国営の小ぎれいなホテルに泊まった。場所柄、時節柄というわけでもなかろうが、宿泊客は、私のほかには、そう多くはなかったように思う。夕食後、ロビーでひとり、コーヒーを飲みながらテレビを見ていると、彼が現れた。わざわざ私が泊まっていたホテルにまで、自作のスライドを持って来てくれたのだ。私は、昼間会った時に訊き漏らしたことはないかと、慎重に思いを巡らしながら、ふたたび彼の話に耳を傾けた。チェーンソーで木を乱暴に切るのは、西欧列強に無理やり引き裂かれたアフリカの歴史の隠喩なのだという。黒い焦げ跡は、同じく植民地支配によって受けたアフリカの人々の精神的な痛みを表し、そして赤や青、黄色の絵の具で書き込まれた記号のような図柄は、そんなアフリカの人々が、太古の時代から受け継いできた父祖伝来の文化を表しているのだという。それは解る。いや、解ると、植民地支配を受けるということがどういうことなのか、肌で知らない私がいうのは、少なくとも言葉の上での説明としては理解できるというのだ。が、私は、アフリカ美術を語る際の、決まり文句といってはいい過ぎだが、そうした使い古された説明とは違うメッセージを私なりに、彼の作品から受け取っていたのである。

エル・アナツイは、今はンスカにある大学の美術教師としてナイジェリアに住んでいるが、もともとは隣国ガーナの生まれである。アシャンティの出身で、古都クマシにある名門クマシ工科大学で美術を学んだ。新生ガーナの美術史の流れでいえば、彼は、アブラデ・グローヴァーよりも一世代あと、いわば第三世代の群像の一人ということができる。もち

Overleaf

The Chips Continue to Fall, 1996

installation, wood
height 260cm, width & depth variable

Photo: Garba Diallo

been delicately picked out in blue and red paints. These were deftly-organised, highly sophisticated works of art.

Almost a year later, at about the time the world was quaking on the verge of the Gulf War, I happened to be in the eastern part of Central Nigeria, where, surrounded by rolling hills, lies the small university town of Nsukka. Since the workshop of the artist whose work had so captivated me the previous year was only a short drive away from the university, I seized upon the opportunity of visiting him in his studio. As I entered the workshop, I was greeted by the fragrant smell of freshly cut wood. There, as he turned on the single bare light illuminating the dark interior, I could see the fine white sawdust blanketing every available surface and carpeting the earth beneath our feet. Then, bringing piece after piece out from the back of the studio, he showed them to me one by one. His work of the time seemed to fall broadly into two distinct types: the first, similar to what I had originally seen in New York, consisted of long, thin, wooden strips hung together to create broad relief panels, the second comprised blocks of wood that had been piled upon each other to a fair height and then had been carved to resemble human figures. I was uncomfortably aware, however, even whilst listening to the artist talking about the different pieces in front of me, that I found it difficult to articulate precisely the impressions that the works produced upon me and the inner feelings they aroused.

I stayed for the night in a small, well-run hotel in Nsukka, which, whether because of its location or because of the time of year, appeared to have almost no other guests that evening besides myself. After supper, just as I was settling down with a cup of coffee in the lobby to watch television, El Anatsui appeared again. He had made his way over to the hotel where I was staying to show me some slides of his work. Thinking to myself that perhaps I had missed something he had been trying to tell me earlier in the day, I once again listened closely to what he was saying.

He explained how he saw in the chainsaw's rough tearing through soft wood a metaphor for the way in which the western powers had carved up and brutally divided the African continent amongst themselves, ripping through and destroying both local history and indigenous culture. Similarly, the scorching of the blackened wood recalled the spiritual injuries and suffering inflicted on the African peoples by the oppression of colonial rule.

Finally, the red, blue and yellow painted marks picking out and illuminating the various symbols and motifs engraved in the wood represented traditional African cultures that have been maintained and transmitted from the ancient times of the ancestors down through successive generations to the present. I thought I understood his words: yet how can someone who has never undergone the experience of colonial oppression ever understand anything but the most superficial meaning of such words? Even so, when describing African art, such explanations — while maybe not quite at the level of cliché — are by no means uncommon, and within myself, I began to sense that his works might carry a different message to his words, and that they might speak to me directly of other concerns.

Though now living in Nigeria, where he holds the post of Head of Sculpture in the Arts Faculty of the University of Nigeria at Nsukka, El Anatsui was actually born in the neighbouring country of Ghana. Born of Ewe stock he first began to study art in earnest at the prestigious University of Science and Technology in Kumasi. From the point of view of Ghanaian contemporary art history, he comes a generation behind Ablade Glover, and can thus be thought of as belonging to the third generation of modern artists produced by that country. One might add that, having been chosen as one of the artists to represent the entire continent of Africa at the 1990 Venice Biennale, he also ranks as one of the more outstanding members of his generation.

ろん、その中でも、1990年にはヴェニス・ビエンナーレに、アフリカ代表の一人として選ばれるなど、彼の活躍は際立っている。

1995年、私は、東京で「インサイド・ストーリー——同時代のアフリカ美術」という展覧会を企画し、その折りに、エル・アナツイにも出品を要請した。私の求めに応じて、アナツイは最新作を2点、ナイジェリアから送ってくれた。そのうちの1点は、ざっくりとした原木を十数体そのまま使った、じつに見応えのあるインスタレーションの大作であった。作品は「あてどなき宿命の旅路」と題されていた(挿図1)。ついでにいうと、この年、彼は同じ日本の大阪で開かれた大阪トリエンナーレにも応募して受賞、その作品が買い上げになり、初めての来日も果たしている。

アナツイの作風は、以前ニューヨークやンスカで見たときとは、少し、けれども明らかに変わっていた。 最初、送られてきた写真を見たとき、私は、ものいいたげな彼のインスタレーションが、何に言い及んでいるのか、はっきりとは了解できないでいた。けれども、実際に展示してみると、すぐにそれがわかった。それほど具体的で、豊かな物語を、彼の作品は、溢れる叙情のうちに奏でていたのである。

西アフリカ一帯では、首都からほんの少し外へ出ると、頭の上に薪を載せた女たちが、縦一列になって道の端を歩いているのをよく目にする。旅行者の目には、何ともアフリカ情趣に溢れた、絵になる風景で、思わずカメラに手がいってしまう瞬間だ。ただ、それはそのように見えるということであって、実際には、熱帯の太陽が容赦なく照りつける中で繰り広げられる女たちの無言の行進は、想像を越える苛酷な労働なのである。女たちは、森で薪を拾い、それを市場まで運んでお金に換えるか、あるいは自分の家に持ち帰って煮炊きに使うかするのだが、いずれにせよ、炎天下の果てしない道のりを、何キロも、何時間も、悪路に足下を取られながら、ひたすら歩き続ける。そうした、アフリカの原風景といってよさそうな女たちを、この彼の作品は描いているのである。そう思ってあらためて見直してみると、中には子どもとおぼしき背の低い者もいるし、あえなく途中で息絶え、置き去りにされてしまった何人かもいる。となると、これは何とも悲しい物語ではないか。彼が題名に含ませた「宿命」という言葉に、ここで一気に歴史の重みが加わってくる。

いうまでもなく、ここでもまた、アナツイはアフリカの歴史を持ち出しているのだ。す

In 1995 I asked El Anatsui to contribute to a touring exhibition that I curated in Tokyo, *An Inside Story: African Art of Our Time.* He responded by sending two of his most recent works from Nigeria, one of which was a large and impressive installation, composed of fifteen or so large pieces of found wood. The piece was named *On Their Fateful Journey Nowhere* (colour plate, pp2-3). That same year, another of his works entered Japan for exhibition as part of the Osaka Triennale, where it won a prize. The work was eventually bought for a Japanese collection, and a subsequent invitation to receive his award in Osaka resulted in the artist's first ever visit to Japan.

Anatsui's work seemed to have changed somewhat from the times when I had first encountered it in New York and again in Nsukka. When I first saw the photographs that he had sent of his installation, the change — though slight — was apparent, though I was still hard put to say exactly what the pieces were trying to say. However when *On Their Fateful Journey Nowhere* was actually set up in the museum, I immediately understood its message. The work told, with a spirited, poetic passion, a richly detailed story.

Throughout West Africa, as soon as you move even a small way outside the large urban centres, you quickly become accustomed to seeing women with bundles of firewood on their heads walking in single file along the roadside. These women present, to the eye of the visitor, such a perfect picture of daily African life that, without thinking, the average tourist will reach for a camera to record the scene. But this picture postcard is no more than the appearance of the moment, for in reality this lengthy carrying of loads of wood under the relentless beating of the tropical sun is actually much more like hard labour. These women gather the firewood in the woods and take it to market to sell, or carry it to their own homes to use for cooking. Whichever is the case, they must walk as many kilometres as it takes, toiling for as many hours as it takes, along difficult roads, and always under the burning sun. It was the exertion of these African women, a primal vision of Africa, that was being portrayed in this installation. Having realised all this, I then looked again at the piece and saw that there were some shorter figures, perhaps children or older people, and several also that seemed to have fallen down and been left behind. What a sad and melancholy story was actually being told here. And, in a single stroke, by his use of the word 'fateful' in the title, the artist had added the entire weight of history to the otherwise common scene.

It hardly needs saying that here was yet another piece by El Anatsui that examined, with a long perspective, the history of Africa and her peoples. The colonial powers of modern Europe wishing to own and control the entire continent of Africa had arbitrarily broken the bonds holding traditional families and societies together and violently divided up the land between themselves. Yet while thus retracing the painful steps of Africa's history, El Anatsui refrains from raising his voice to condemn the western powers of the present day, demanding an equal revenge for the violence visited on his people, exacting an eye for an eye, or otherwise requiring that further blood be spilt in atonement. Instead he presents, with telling simplicity, the figure of these women, an abiding image familiar to all Africans from the earliest memories of their childhood. These women tell a far richer story, one that expresses a timeless reality tinged with deeper human truths than all the written histories contain. The history books, at best, describe only how the European — one might almost say the Christian — powers attempted to dominate and control this other continent. In the scene as it now unfolds before us, the women, witnesses to the real truths of time and place — truths that are never told in the western history books — step forward on the stage together, like an ancient chorus, to sing:

べてを支配し、所有しないではいられない近代ヨーロッパの植民地主義によって、理不尽に襲断され、伝統的な家族や地域の絆を暴力的に引き裂かれてしまったアフリカ。そのアフリカの悲痛な歴史を踏まえながら、しかしエル・アナツイは、自分と同時代の西欧に対して、声高に非難するのでもなく、かつて自分たちが受けたのと同じ暴力の刃を向けて、血で血を洗う報復を企てようとするのでもない。ただひたすら愚直に、アフリカ人ならだれでも幼いころから知っている女たちの姿を、提示し続けるのである。その女たちはといえば、ヨーロッパ的な、あえていえばキリスト教的な、支配と所有の欲望が織り上げたのとは違う、おそらくはもっと豊かな物語を、悠遠なる詩情のうちに謳い上げるのだ。女たちは、このとき、ヨーロッパが書き上げた近代史とは別の、もうひとつの歴史の語り部として、私たちの前に立ち現れるのである。

北の諸国に翻弄されてさまよえるアフリカは、このあとどこへ流れていくのかわからない。けれども、旅する私たちは、いつでも必要最低限のものだけを身にまとい、それ以上を望まない。まして、異教の人々を、神の愛の名の下に支配し、所有しようなどとは思わない。そのことを貧しいと、私たちは思わない。豊かさというものが、他者を支配し、所有することによってしか得られないのなら、そんな豊かさなど、私たちは望みはしない・・。女たちの歌が、私の耳にはそんな風に聞こえてくる。

アナツイが旧英領の出身だという点を捉えて、彼の作品を、たとえば現代イギリスの自然主義的な彫刻の流れの中に置こうとするならば、それはあまりにも粗雑で浅薄な行為だというべきであろう。彼の作品は、一見、アートという文法に取り込まれているかのようにみえるが、じつは、アートという名のイデオロギーと、その背後にある西欧近代そのものへの静かな、その分だけ有効な批判になりえているのである。

After such shameful treatment
at the hands of other countries lying far to the North,
Africa has lost its bearings
And is now adrift.

We cannot tell what lies ahead.
Carrying with us only
The bare necessities of life
We are content as we journey on
And do not wish for more.

We have no dreams of dominion
No hidden schemes
To conquer people with other creeds
Subjecting them to the rule of love
Of a jealous god.

If riches and wealth can only be had
By taking what belongs to others —
We have no desire for riches so obtained.
Though we may seem impoverished
We know that we are not *that* poor.

This is the song the women sang softly to my ears, as I stood before the piece, wrapped in contemplation.

Although El Anatsui was raised in a former British colony, it must be realised that his work differs markedly from and cannot properly be compared to the work of other contemporary British sculptors, even those, for example, who might work with natural materials and found objects. Though El Anatsui's work, at first sight, appears to exist within the boundaries of contemporary 'western art,' and therefore to be subject to criticism by its rules and ordinary tools of analysis, yet the work, as in this example, serves as a searching indictment and a quiet reproof of the whole notion of 'art' and the bedrock of ideological certainty upon which it rests. In this crucial sense we can see El Anatsui employing the common idioms and grammar of contemporary western art at the same time as he actively undermines them by introducing and juxtaposing ideas, techniques and material from never yet subjugated areas that lie far beyond the pale of western art.

— *Translated by Gerard Houghton*

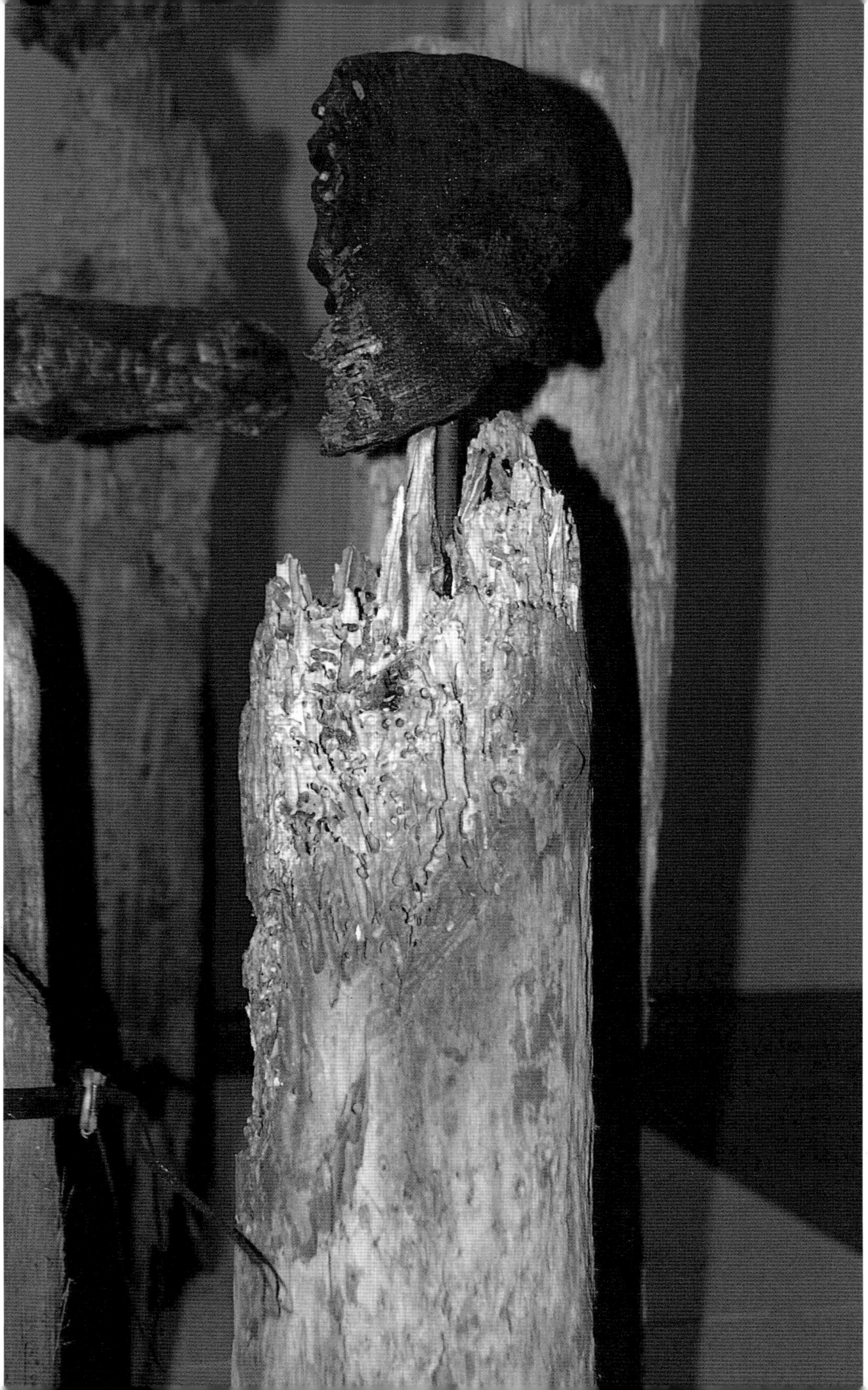

Akua's Surviving Children, 1996 (detail)

installation, found wood & metal
height 165cm, width & depth variable

Photo: El Anatsui

Colour plate on pp38-39

ELISABETH LALOUSCHEK

Ein Künstler der Transvangarde: Weltansichten und Weltgeschichten

Ich betrachte El Anatsui als einen der wesentlichen und bedeutensten gegenwärtigen Künstler Afrikas. Seine gebrannten, mit elektrischer Motorsäge zerschnittenen und mit Tempera bemalten Arbeiten stehen als mächtige Metaphern für die afrikanische Geschichte. Seine Ahnenfiguren, die teilweise bemalt und geschnitzt sind, und aus alten Hauspfosten geformt, die der Künstler in verlassenen Behausungen fand, strahlen den Geist alter afrikanischer Skulpturen aus. Seine großen Installationen aus altem, von der Zeit gezeichnetem Holz, verbinden den Geist afrikanischer Kunst mit Denkformen gegenwärtiger westlicher Kunst. In einer Ausstellung in New York wurden die Werke El Anatsuis denen Sol LeWitts gegenübergestellt, woraus sich ein spannender Dialog zwischen zwei einander überschneidenden Ideen- und Formwelten ergab.[1]

[1] *El Anatsui & Sol LeWitt*, Skoto Gallery, New York, 1996.

Erste Begegnung

Ich erinnere mich noch sehr gut an den Nachmittag, an dem ich El Anatsui entdeckte. Gemeinsam mit Chili Hawes, Direktorin in der October Gallery und Adrian Plant von der Tate Gallery, Liverpool, schaute ich mir die Video-Dokumentation: *Kindred Spirits: Gegenwärtige Nigerianische Künstler,* produziert von der Smithsonian World, USA an. Und plötzlich sah ich, wie sich eine Motorsäge kraftvoll durch tropisches Hartholz fraß. Das Geräusch der Motorsäge

Elisabeth Lalouschek, born in Vienna, is the Artistic Director of the October Gallery. She holds an MA in Fine Art from the Royal College of Art and received the Elizabeth Greenshield Award in 1980, a British Council scholarship 1981-83 and the George Rowney Bicentennial Special Award in 1983. As the Artistic Director of the October Gallery, she has curated numerous exhibitions of contemporary art from around the world and has offered her expertise to individuals and institutions worldwide. She co-ordinated the London end of An Inside Story: African Art of our Time, *an exhibition of contemporary African art touring six museums in Japan, which started at the Setagaya Art Museum, Tokyo, in September 1995. In 1997 she organised two major consecutive exhibitions at the October Gallery on the work of international artists of Yoruba culture, entitled* Yoruba Diasporas.

war ohrenbetäubend, dann wurde das Holz schwarz gebrannt. Ich wurde Zeugin der Erschaffung eines Meisterwerks gegenwärtiger Kunst. Dieser Künstler mußte gefunden werden. Ich begann London nach Arbeiten von El Anatsui zu durchforsten. Und dann, eines Tages, rief Sandor Péri an, ein ungarischer Architekt. Er besaß mehrere Arbeiten des Künstlers, von frühen Holztafeln über Wandreliefs bis hin zu frei stehenden Skulpturen. Sandor Péri war einer der hauptverantwortlichen Planer für die neue *Universität von Nigeria* in Nsukka gewesen. 1982 hatte er den Wissenschaftsblock gebaut, für den er zwei öffentliche Skulpturen von El Anatsui, welcher einige Jahre vorher an der Universität zu unterrichten begonnen hatte, in Auftrag gab. So kam es, daß El Anatsui 1993 zum ersten Mal in der October Gallery in der Ausstellung *Six African Artists* ausstellte. Im September/Oktober 1995 erfolgte an der October Gallery auch seine erste Einzelausstellung in Großbritannien.

Die October Gallery eröffnete 1979, um Künstler der *Transvangarde* auszustellen und bekannt zu machen. Im Laufe ihrer Geschichte hat die Galerie Künstler aller Kontinente ausgestellt. In ihren *Transvangarde*-Ausstellungen stellt sie die Arbeiten der besten Künstler einander gegenüber, um so einen dynamischen internationalen Dialog visueller Denkformen zu erzeugen. Die *Transvangarde* kann am besten als transkulturelle Avantgarde definiert werden. Sie ist ein Experiment, das sich in ständiger Entwicklung befindet, und kann nur im Zusammenhang mit einer weltweit aktiven gegenwärtigen Kunstszene gesehen werden. *Transvangarde* ist Kunst auf des Messers Schneide, sie handelt von Risiko und unerwartetem Neuen. Sie ist der Stoff, aus dem die große gegenwärtige Kunst gemacht wird, und El Anatsui ist ein perfektes Beispiel dafür: in der einen Hand hält er die Ideen und Formen Afrikas und in der anderen Hand die gängigen Ideen der westlichen Avantgarde. Beim Bildhauen verwendet er beide Hände und wird zum Meister zweier verschiedener Welten. Die daraus entstehenden Arbeiten bewegen sich anstrengungslos zwischen afrikanischen und westlichen ästhetischen Empfindungen und können von beiden gelesen werden. "Nur wenn man von einer Position klaren Wissens und Definition seiner selbst aus arbeitet, hat man die Möglichkeit, etwas Bedeutungsvolles zu einer wie auch immer aussehenden, neu entstehenden Kulturformation beizutragen,"[2] sagt El Anatsui.

Dichter mit Motorsäge

Slash rip sear whittle
devastate chip chop
break burn impose juxtapose
control
Express new ideas in old wood. Mix time-furrowed
experience with buoyant smoothness; the concavity of old time with the convex
posture of new time.
New wood has poetry locked in it.
Old wood is poetry itself, time
Having worn off its prose.[3]

Eines von El Anatsuis wichtigsten Themen ist die Geschichte Afrikas: die Sklaverei, die Wanderungen, Vertreibungen und Enteignungen seiner vielen Völker und das heutige Erbe dieser Geschehnisse. Er verwendet die Motorsäge, um seine kraftvollen Visionen ins Holz zu schneiden. Er formt und bezeichnet tropisches Hartholz, er ritzt Kerben hinein und reißt und

[2] 'Sankofa: Go Back an' Pick' in *Three Studio Notes and a Conversation: Conversation with Olu Oguibe. Third Text* (London: Kala Press, Nummer 23, 1993), Seite 49.

[3] Aufschlitzen zerreiflen versengen abschaben/ verwüsten abhacken kleinhacken/ brechen brennen aufbürden nebeneinanderstellen/ kontrollieren
Drücke neue Ideen in altem Holz aus. Vermische zeit-durchfurchte/ Erfahrung mit lebhafter Glätte; die Einwölbung alter Zeit mit der nach außen gewölbten/ Haltung der neuen Zeit
Neues Holz hat Dichtung in sich eingeschloßen,/ Altes Holz ist Dichtung selbst, Zeit,/ die ihre Prosa abgetragen hat.
—*Old and New*, exhibition catalogue, Lagos, 1991.

brennt es. Die Holzsorten, die er verwendet, stehen als Metaphern für Gewebe, Fasern, Farbe und Muster afrikanischer Geschichte. Die elektrische Säge reißt das Holz willkürlich auseinander, so wie Afrika willkürlich in Kolonien zerissen wurde. Geschichte erstreckt sich in El Anatsuis Arbeiten auch auf die Gegenwart. Die Völkerwanderungen, Sklaverei und Enteignungen sind für ihn nicht abgeschloßene Ereignisse, sie spielen sich auch noch in den verschiedensten Verkleidungen in der Gegewart ab.

In vielen Arbeiten kombiniert El Anatsui Formen, Motive und Symbole von Ewe und Ashanti Streifengeweben mit *Uli*[4], *Nsibidi*[5], *Adinkra*[6] und andere Designs. Er sucht auch nach Symbolen und Schriftzeichen diverser afrikanischer Kulturen, die er kombiniert, und entgegnet damit den Behauptungen, Afrika hätte keine Schrifttradition. "Die Schriftzeichen seiner Völker zu erforschen, gibt Einblick in deren abstraktes Denken und in die Formen ihrer Verbildlichung," sagt der Künstler.[7]

El Anatsuis Reliefs bestehen aus einzelnen Hölzern, deren Reihenfolge in der Zusammensetzung auswechselbar ist. In seinen jüngsten Arbeiten verwendete El Anatsui Schwemmholz, alte Hauspfosten und das alte Holz von Mörsern. Diese wurden früher dafür verwendet, Palmöl zu extrahieren, sind aber jetzt mit ihren, vom Schlagen verbrauchten Böden, weggeworfen worden. Der Mörser wird rekonstruiert, aber seine letztendliche Form bleibt von vergangenen Erfahrungen geprägt, seine Geschichte wird manifest gemacht und nicht verkleidet.

Traditionelle Holzschnitzer mußten den Geistern des Holzes Gebete und Opfer darbringen, bevor sie beim Bäumefällen den ersten Schlag mit der Axt setzten. Denn jeder Baumstamm hat eine Seele oder eine ihm innewohnende geistige Kraft, und der Künstler steht mit ihr in direkter Verbindung und fühlt die Form der Seele des Holzes. Bildhauerei wird ein geheiligter Akt. Installationen und Aufführungen sind Dinge, mit denen Afrikaner immer gelebt haben und die für sie selbstverständlich sind. Es gibt Installationen, die man in jedem Dorfplatz antrifft, Schreine und Altäre, denen man tagtäglich begegnet, oder seltene, saisongebundene Installationen und Aufführungen, wie die Igbo Mbari[8] und Ijele[9], oder die mehrere Kilometer lange Wasserschlangen Maskerade der Kalabari. Daß diese Manifestationen immer noch ihre evokative Macht behalten haben, liegt vermutlich daran, daß ihre Schaffung nur ausgewählten Künstlern und in manchen Fällen eingeweihten Künstlern erlaubt ist.

Eine von El Anatsuis jüngsten Installationen, *Akua's Surviving Children* (Farbabb. Seite 38f.) ist aus dänischem Treibholz gemacht. 1996 war El Anatsui eingeladen worden, eine Arbeit für das Festival *Images of Africa* in Dänemark zu konzipieren. Ein Schwerpunkt dieses Festivals bildete die Rückschau auf das dänische Sklaverei-Projekt, das von 1670 — 1850 zwischen der ehemaligen Goldküste (jetzt Ghana) und den dänischen Westindischen Inseln (jetzt die US-Jungferninseln) durchgeführt worden war. El Anatsui beschreibt, was nach Wochen der Suche nach dem richtigen Standort und der richtigen Inspiration passierte: "Ein einzelnes Stück Treibholz lag auf dem Strand von Hellebaek, irgendwo im nördlichsten Teil von Dänemark. Als ich die steilen Stufen zum Meer hinunterstieg und das Stück Holz aufstellte, waren seine erzählenden Merkmale von Stimmungen geladen. Abgesehen davon, daß es von Meer und Wetter durch eine lange Zeit hindurch herumgeworfen und geformt worden war, steckte in ihm eine rostige Eisenstange oder ein Stück einer Verankerungskette. Ich ließ es stehen und ging weg.

Bei meinem zweiten Besuch am Strand waren zwei weitere Stämme angeschwemmt worden, und ich stellte sie sofort daneben. Ein Klan von Überlebenden begann sich zu bilden. Ich glaube, daß sich von da an ein Zusammenhang, der sich früher schon angedeuted hatte, verstärkte. An

[4]Ein Korpus von Motiven, das von den Igbo in Körper und Wandmalerei verwendet wird.

[5]Ein Geheimcode, der übersetzt werden kann, und der von der Leopard (Ekpe) Gesellschaft im südöstlichen Nigeria verwendet wird.

[6]Akan schwarz bestempelte Stoffdesigns.

[7]'Slashing Wood, Eroding Culture: Conversation with El Anatsui.' El Anatsui im Interview mit Chika Okeke. *NKA Journal of Contemporary African Art* (New York, Issue 1, Herbst/Winter 1994) Seite 35.

[8]Igbo Mbari Häuser werden als Opferstellen für örtliche Götter gebaut. Es ist wichtig, daß sie eindrucksvolle und sorgfältig gemachte Kunstwerke darstellen.

[9]Die massive Ijele Maske der Igbo ist eine prächtige, symbolische Struktur, die nur von einem Individuum mit großer Stärke getanzt werden kann.

den darauffolgenden Tagen durchquerte ich mehrere Kilometer des Strands und entdeckte fast dreißig Mitglieder dieses Klans, welche alle gerettet und in mein Atelier in der Hammermill gebracht wurden, für das, was ich ein Ritual der Erneuerung nennen würde: ich brannte im Ofenfeuer die Gesichter der Köpfe, und befestigte sie mit in der Schmiede handgemachten Nägeln."

Vor über dreihundert Jahren war die Hammermill in Hellebaek eine Waffenfabrik. Als Schmiede produzierte sie Gewehrläufe, die abgesehen von anderen Verwendungszwecken im dänischen Sklavenprojekt eingesetzt wurden. Jetzt wurde sie renoviert, und dient mit ihren Nachbildungen von vom Wasser angetriebenen schweren Hämmern als Museum, wo Schmiede den oft und zahlreich kommenden Besuchern die Arbeitsabläufe vorführen. El Anatsui beschloß, an diesem Ort wegen seiner historischen Verbindungen zu arbeiten. Um seine Skulpturen herzustellen, benutzte er die gleichen Geräte, die für die Herstellung von Waffen verwendet wurden, als ein Akt der Umkehrung und symbolischen Reinigung.

Für El Anatsui waren folgende Handlungen und Entscheidungen bestimmend: Die Umstände, denen Treibholz ausgesetzt ist, entsprechen der Situation von Sklaven: Treibholz wird aus seinem Heimatland gerissen und in die feindliche See geworfen, wird herumgeschleudert, und kommt letztendes ans Land zurück, mit den Erlebnissen seines Leidenswegs. Die große Anzahl der Stücke in *Akua's Surviving Children* entspricht der Sklaverei, die ja mit großen Zahlen zutun hatte, und nicht mit den einzelnen Individuen. Das Individuum wurde statistisch reduziert.

Die Köpfe der Figuren sind verbrannt, denn das Verbrennen ist ein Ritual der Reinigung, das immer noch in einigen Teilen der Gesellschaft ausgeübt wird. Zudem vollendet das Feuer als letztes Element den Erlebniszyklus des Holzes, dadurch daß das Holz, selbst aus Erde geboren, vorher schon den Elementen des Wassers und des Windes ausgesetzt war. Der Titel identifiziert das Werk mit einem bestimmten Standort, nämlich mit der Goldküste (Ghana), das Land des Fruchtbarkeitsymbols *Akua-ba* (Akua's Kind). Zahlen, die groß genug sind, um eine Statistik zu ermöglichen, können nur aus einem fruchtbaren Ursprung stammen.

Künstler in der Geschichte

El Anatsui wurde 1944 in Anyako, im südöstlichen Ghana geboren. Er studierte Bildhauerei an der Universität für Wissenschaft und Technologie in Kumasi. Er spürte, daß die Ausbildung, die er erhielt, und welche zum größten Teil auf westlichen Kunsttechniken basierte, nicht nur inadäquat, sondern geradezu entfremdend war. Deshalb begann er eine persönliche Suche zur Reorientierung seiner künstlerischen Perspektive. An Wochenenden besuchte er das Nationale Kulturzentrum in Kumasi, wo er Handwerkern beim Weben, Stoffdrucken, Schnitzen, Bronzegiessen und anderen Arbeiten zusah, oder einfach die reichen Klänge von Musikorchestern bei deren Aufführung oder Probe genoß. Viele dieser Handwerker verwendeten *Adinkra* Symbole. Von 1969 an unterrichtete El Anatsui in der Kunsterziehungsabteilung im Specialist Training College in Winneba. 1970 begann El Anatsui an einer Serie von Holztafeln zu arbeiten. Die Marktfrauen in Winneba verwendeten kreisförmige Holztablette, in die Designs gebrannt waren. Er bestellte Tablette von den Schnitzern, in die er seine eigenen Designs brannte. 1975 verließ El Anatsui Ghana und nahm eine Stelle an der Universität von Nigeria in Nsukka an, wo er seitdem unterrichtet. Dort traf er Uche Okeke, der 1958 die Zaria Art Society gegründet hatte. Diese vertrat die Theorie der *Natürlichen Synthese (Natural Synthesis),* die zur Vermischung der besten einheimischen Kunsttraditionen, Formen und Ideen mit nützlichen westlichen aufrief. El Anatsui empfand dies als wichtig für seine eigenen Arbeitsmethoden. Er begann das wesentliche lokale Idiom *Uli* in seine Arbeit zu integrieren, und fühlte sich auch von zwei Skulpturtraditionen angezogen, den Steinmonolithen von Akwanshi[10] und den Nok[11] Terracotta-Skulpturen.

[10] Einfache Steinmonolithen, in die sparsam geometrische Muster eingraviert sind.

[11] Die Skulpturen der Nok Kultur aus Nigeria sind die ältesten bekannten Skulpturen Afrikas, abgesehen von Ägypten.

Zwischen 1976 und 1982 arbeitete er auch in Ton (z B *Broken Pots* Serie). Er begann an Workshops und Ausstellungen im Ausland teilzunehmen. 1980 arbeitete er in der Cummington Community of Arts, Massachusetts, wo er begann, die elektrische Säge als Schnitzwerkzeug zu verwenden; 1984 nahm er am *Zweiten Symposium Nordseeküste*, Cuxhaven, Deutschland, teil; 1990 repräsentierte er Afrika in der *Venedig Biennale*; 1992 beteiligte er sich mit Künstlern wie Anthony Gormley und Marina Abramovic an dem *Arte Amazonas* Projekt in Rio de Janeiro, wo er eines seiner Hauptwerke *Erosion* produzierte, welches im Rahmen der Austellung *Klima Global* 1993 zur Staatlichen Kunsthalle, Berlin, und 1994 zum Ludwig Forum, Aachen, Deutschland, kam. 1995 nahm er an der *Configura 2* in Erfurt, Deutschland, teil, ebenso wie an der Wanderausstellung *An Inside Story: African Art of Our Time*, die in sechs Museen in Japan zu sehen war, und die am Setagaya Art Museum, Tokio, Japan, begann; schließlich stellte er in der Ausstellung *Seven Stories about Modern Art in Africa* in der Whitechapel Art Gallery, London, UK, aus. 1995 hatte er seine erste Einzelausstellung in der October Gallery, London. 1996 nahm er an der Ausstellung *Container 96* in Kopenhagen teil und stellte gemeinsam mit Sol LeWitt in der Skoto Gallery, New York, aus. 1997/98 wurde er in der Austellung *The Poetics of Line: Seven Artists of the Nsukka Group* am National Museum of African Art, Washington DC, USA, gezeigt und 1998 in einer weiteren Einzelausstellung in der October Gallery, London. Seine großen Erfolge erweisen El Anatsui als einen der großen Künstler unserer Zeit, der mit seinen kraftvollen Werken, die Welten verbinden, Geschichte macht.

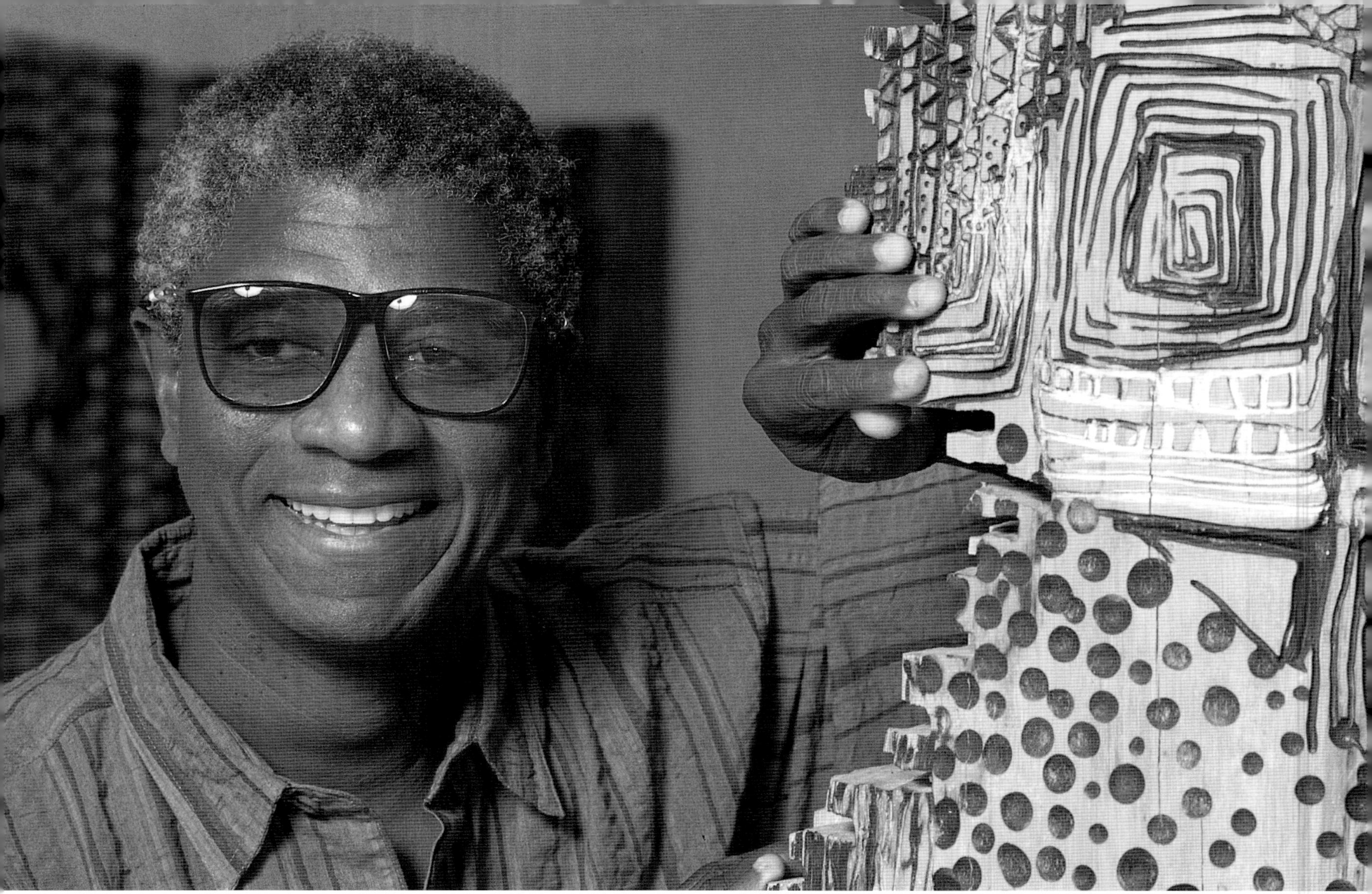

El Anatsui at the October Gallery with Erosion, *1995*

Photo: Andy Keate

SIMON NJAMI

Un artiste sur le fil de l'histoire

Collage et Permanence

La notion d'artiste est une invention récente. Le sculpteur Benvenuto Cellini — orfèvre, médailleur italien du XVIe siècle, auteur entre autres chefs d'œuvre de *La Nymphe de Fontainebleau* et du *Persée de la Loggia*, ne se définissait-il pas lui-même comme un artisan? Jusqu'à la Renaissance et même au-delà, l'on ne pouvait séparer le peintre ou le sculpteur de la Création et du Créateur de toute chose. L'art fut de tout temps lié à un Dieu et il a fallu notre siècle pour venir à bout de cette célébration à la fois implicite et explicite. Un regard attentif nous indiquerait d'ailleurs que l'homme n'a pas tué Dieu. C'est la civilisation industrielle qui est parvenue à cette improbable séparation freudienne. Et dès lors que la sacralité s'était mise à fuir le monde industrialisé, les pays où la technologie n'avait pas encore pris un essor hégémonique ont hérité de la lourde charge de représenter à eux seuls toute la charge spirituelle du monde. L'homme à l'état de nature — ou plutôt, pour éviter toute sorte de malentendus, l'homme dans sa nature — a le sentiment justifié de participer d'un tout. De concourir à l'équilibre d'un ensemble qu'il ne maîtrise pas, un ensemble transcendant dont, pourtant, il a l'intime conviction d'être l'un des rouages les plus précieux.

C'est donc en toute logique que celui que nous désignons aujourd'hui par le mot 'artiste' fut d'abord et avant tout un *homo faber,* qui remplissait une fonction précise dans la société, comme

Simon Njami was born in Lausanne, Switzerland, of Cameroonian parents. He holds PhDs in both Modern Literature and Law (Paris) and is a Visiting Professor at the Visual Arts Department, University of San Diego, California. A co-founder and the Chief Editor of Revue Noire, *the French magazine dealing with contemporary African art, he has published several books of his own including the novel* African Gigolo *(Seghers 1989) and a biography of James Baldwin,* Le Devoir de Violence *(Seghers, 1991). Besides these literary achievements he has also made his mark in the field of the visual arts, as an artist in his own right, with exhibitions such as* Ethnicolour, *Paris 1987 and* Die Andere Reise, *Krems, Austria, 1996, as well as working as a scriptwriter. He is currently at work on a biography of Leopold Sedar Senghor and a novel,* An Ink Memory, *both to be published by Le Seuil, Paris.*

nous le confirme El Anatsui. “There is a peculiarity about the artist. He could be more sensitive, could be a visionary, could have higher imaginative powers, but he is, unlike the Messiah, essentially a member of his community who suffers the same fate as any other. I do not think anything is expected of him at all costs — his peculiar endowments make him do what he does: to sensitise society so that it might stabilise itself or, if you like, save itself, including the artist. He does not try to win them over as followers or worshippers, only vaguely hopes to provoke their active participation in a self-redeeming process. Because he is a member of the society, we tend to talk about and assess his relevance to that society and that generation — every generation has its own artists.”[1]

Ce n’est que lorsque l’artisan a été séparé de la société qu’est apparu l’artiste et, avec lui, notre conception moderne de l’art. Cette séparation qui renforçait l’individu au dépens du groupe, l’Afrique a d˚ attendre le vingtième siècle pour l’opérer. Je suis néanmoins convaincu que nombre d’entre les artistes africains les plus signifiants de notre siècle se sont d’abord définis comme des artisans, des éléments d’une chaine sociale et pour eux, l’idée selon laquelle l’artiste est un être qui vit en dehors du monde était une hérésie. El Anatsui est sans aucun doute à mettre au nombre de ceux-là.

La leçon que nous donne depuis quelques années l’art contemporain africain, l’art contemporain tout court, est que tout art est nécessairement le fruit d’un processus de collage et de permanence. “ The subject matter of art itself, life, has rarely changed over the ages, and that process of renewal, the new ways of presenting the same old materials, is what kept it going.”[2] Elle part du principe que la nature fondamentale de l’être humain, son essence première est immuable. Ce qui ne signifie en aucun cas que cette nature soit figée. Le principe de collage est cette opération de sédimentation qui nous fabrique au quotidien et nous rend, d’un jour l’autre, la fois semblable et différent. Nous sommes les sujets de notre temps, et mêmes les Inuit du nord du Canada sont branchés sur internet. Au centre de la création, qu’elle soit plastique ou naturelle est l’homme. Et le plus grand défi auquel il nous ait été donné de faire face est d’être capable de donner de nous-mêmes une définition qui engloberait, sans exclusive, l’ensemble de ce qui nous fait être.

L’injonction qui ornait le frontispice du temple de Delphes au temps des grecs anciens, le fameux ‘connais-toi toi-même,’ est plus que jamais, à l’heure d’une mondialisation qui menace d’imposer de nouvelles hégémonies, d’actualité. Relisant Hegel, Césaire affirmait que l’universalisme ne saurait être rien d’autre que la somme des particularités. Nous sommes ces particularités. Ces éléments complexes, ces atomes insignifiants sans lesquels il ne saurait y avoir de véritable humanité, comprise au sens d’universalité. C’est la raison pour laquelle la plongée au sein de sa propre histoire, de son expérience individuelle devient indispensable à quiconque prétend vouloir créer et transmettre à autrui ce qu’il a compris du monde. Elle est la pierre angulaire qui seule nous permet d’absorber l’autre, de nous nous nourrir de l’autre. “As for hybridity, the hybridisation of cultures, as of now, is to me more of a conjecture than reality. I do not buy the idea of universal culture. Every culture has its essence which, like the soul of man, you cannot change or infect easily. People may talk about a universal culture, a hybrid world culture, because there is greater and faster dissemination of knowledge across boundaries. I read recently about one American scholar talking about a ‘multi-versal’ instead of a ‘uni-versal’ culture. Whatever the case may be, it is from virile stock that a farmer selects to create a hybrid. Unless a culture has strength, it cannot contribute effectively to a universal, or multiversal, dispensation, and that, perhaps, is why it is dangerous for an artist easily to throw away his cultural heirloom and superficially take on an alien one. Any such artist has no confidence in his own and his work is unlikely to be viable or virile, and thus irrelevant

[1] Anatsui, El, ‘Sankofa: Go Back an’ Pick. Three Studio Notes and a Conversation,’ *Third Text: Third World Perspectives on Contemporary Art and Culture*, No 23 Summer, p52, London: Kala Press, 1993. “Il y a quelque chose de particulier chez l’artiste. Il se pourrait qu’il soit plus sensible, qu’il soit un visionnaire, que ses pouvoirs d’imagination soient supérieurs, mais il est essentiellement, à la différence du Messie, un membre de sa communauté qui connaît le même destin que les autres. Je ne crois pas que l’on attende quelque chose de lui à tout prix — ce sont ses dons particuliers qui lui font faire ce qu’il fait: sensibiliser la société, peut la stabiliser, ou mieux, la sauver, y compris l’artiste lui-même. Il ne tente pas de s’attacher les membres de sa communauté comme des disciples ou des admirateurs lui vouant un culte, il se contente d’espérer provoquer une participation active de leur part à un processus de rédemption personnelle. Parce qu’il est membre d’une société, nous avons tendance à nous référer et à juger son adéquation à sa société et à sa génération — chaque génération engendrant ses propres artistes.”

[2] Ibid, p41. “Le sujet de l’art en soi, la vie, n’a guère changé au cours des siècles, et ce processus de renouvellement, les nouvelles façons de présenter les matériaux du passé, c’est ce qui l’a fait aller de l’avant.”

It is only when one proceeds from a position of clear knowledge and definition of oneself that one stands a bright chance of contributing meaningfully to whatever culture formation eventually emerges."[3] "Picasso n'a pas agi autrement devant le masque du Musée de l'Homme de Paris. Il s'est soudain trouvé confronté à une expérience qui trouvait des résonnances dans les profondeurs de son moi. Ce masque fondateur n'a été qu'un élément déclencheur d'une vision qui couvait en lui depuis toujours. Ne restait plus qu'à le façonner, à l'absorber, à l'ingérer jusqu'au point où il deviendrait une part inamovible de lui-même. Collage.

C'est ainsi, donc, que le processus créateur, de tout temps, n'aura jamais été que la reproduction revisitée par notre état présent, par notre expérience remise à jour, de ce que notre bagage génétique, culturel et social aura inscrit en nous dès notre plus jeune âge. Un bagage qui aura dû, au fil des générations, passer par des altérations parfois subtiles, parfois brutales. Il n'y a pas, dès lors, de création sans mémoire. Mais le souvenir ne signifie pas, loin s'en faut, la reproduction fidèle et laborieuse d'un modèle donné comme référence absolue. Cette mémoire procède bien plutôt par oblitération, par reconstitution, par re-création. Ce que le professeur Toshome Gabriel a appelé les ruines. Ces ruines constituent notre mémoire hallucinée, notre mémoire idéale, en quelque sorte, qui repose moins sur les faits concrets que sur une intuition, une sensation, une sensualité qui varient d'un sujet à l'autre, et nous rend capable d'être des animaux créateurs. Des inventeurs. L'artiste est celui qui réinvente sa mémoire au jour le jour. Qui réécrit sans cesse son histoire et celle des siens. Usant d'une langue et d'images qui n'existaient pas.

Histoire, Mémoire et Tradition

"When I last wrote you about Africa/I used a letter-headed parchment paper/There were many blank slots in the letter.../I can now fill some of these slots because.../I have grown older."[4] Que veut donc nous dire Anatsui à travers ces quelques lignes? De quoi veut-il nous parler si ce n'est de notre histoire? De son histoire? Cette Afrique à laquelle il fait référence, il avoue ne commencer à la comprendre qu'à l'heure où il rédige ces lignes. Sa connaissance, jusqu'alors, était faite de passages vides, de trous, qu'il lui incombait de combler à travers l'expérience initiatique la plus forte: la vie. Et à mesure que se remplissent les passages en blanc, il réalise qu'il a vieilli. Mais non pas au sens physique du terme. Au sens spirituel. Il a mûri. Les atouts avec lesquels nous naissons nous sont bien inintelligibles. Nous n'avons pas les armes nécessaires pour déchiffrer l'indéchiffrable. Et c'est le chemin que nous suivons qui nous éclaire sur celui qu'il nous reste à parcourir. Pour Anatsui, on pourrait distinguer trois ou quatre étapes dans cette quête du sens. La première, la fondatrice, est Anyako, au Ghana. Le centre tellurique de l'âme du sculpteur. Son père est un tisserand. Il se souvient des différents chefs de village et sans doute, du métier, au sens premier du terme, de son père. Puis vient le temps de l'école qui constitue une rupture, même si, selon Chike C Aniakor, le collège et le lycée ne laisseront aucun souvenir indélébile dans l'âme du futur sculpteur. On a peine à croire qu'un système scolaire en rupture avec les habitudes familiales, pendant une période où la colonisation anglaise, qui ne devait prendre fin que le 6 mars 1957, vivait ses dernières années n'ait pas eu plus d'effet que cela sur l'enfant qu'était Anatsui. Il n'est pas à douter, au contraire, que cette période de scolarité ait laissé des traces qui devaient remonter plus tard à la surface, dans l'affirmation forte d'une identité revendiquée. Il y avait dès lors l'Histoire, celle qu'on lui enseignait à l'école, et les histoires, celles que son père et ceux de son village, les chefs, avaient commencé de lui transmettre. Puis vient le temps de l'université. Autre rupture. Autres initiations sur le chemin de la découverte. Autres collages. Des études d'art, une spécialisation en sculpture. Après l'obtention de ses diplômes, il

[3]ibid, p49."En ce qui concerne le processus actuel d'hybridation des cultures, cela tient plus pour moi de la conjecture que de la réalité. Je n'adhère pas à la notion de culture universelle. Chaque culture possède son essence propre que, telle l'âme humaine, on ne peut aisément transformer ou infecter. On a beau jeu de parler d'une culture universelle, d'une culture mondiale hybride, en raison d'une propagation plus étendue et plus rapide des connaissances par-delà les frontières. J'ai lu récemment qu'un universitaire américain se référait volontiers à une culture 'multi-verselle' plutôt 'qu'uni-verselle.' Quoi qu'il en soit, c'est à partir d'une souche vigoureuse que le paysan opère sa sélection en vue de créer un hybride. Si une culture est dépourvue de vigueur, elle ne peut apporter une contribution efficace à un développement universel ou multiversel et c'est peut-être la raison pour laquelle il est dangereux pour un artiste de se débarrasser trop vite de son héritage culturel pour endosser un autre vernis culturel qui lui reste étranger. Un tel artiste n'a pas confiance en lui et il est peu probable que son travail soit viable ou animé d'un force virile; il est donc dépourvu de sens. Ce n'est qu'en se fondant sur une connaissance et une définition claire de soi que l'artiste a de grandes chances de contribuer de façon significative à l'émergence d'une quelconque gestation culturelle."

[4]Aniakor, C C, 'El Anatsui: Visual Incantations in Wood,' *The International Review of African American Art*, 9, no3."La dernière fois où je t'ai écrit au sujet de l'Afrique / j'avais utilisé un papier à lettre artisanal à entète / il y a avait de nombreux blancs dans cette lettre.../je suis maintenant en mesure de remplir certains de ces blancs parce que.../ j'ai mûri avec l'âge."

devient professeur et connaît son premier choc esthétique conscient. Une découverte qui, d'emblée, remet en cause les fondements d'une formation académique par trop détachée du réel: sur les marchés, les femmes disposaient leurs marchandises sur des plateaux en bois ciselé qui étaient décorés à l'aide d'une technique de pirogravure. Ainsi, la vérité, le sens de sa recherche avait-elle toujours été devant ses yeux, mais il lui fallait la maturité pour être capable de voir.

En 1975, Anatsui est engagé à l'université de Nsukka, au Nigéria. Autre étape, autre déplacement, autre choc: les monolithes Akwanshi dans la cour du Musée National de Lagos, les terres cuites Nok et, pour finir, la peinture corporelle Igbo, connue sous le nom de *Uli*. La dernière étape de cette longue quête, de cette recherche du langage parfaitement adapté aura lieu en 1980 aux Etats-Unis, à Cummington, Massachusetts, avec la découverte des ressources esthétiques et calligraphiques de la tronçonneuse. C'est lesté de tous ces éléments, de toutes ces découvertes et de toutes ces aventures, tous ces voyages sur lesquels il n'est pas utile de revenir, que El Anatsui pourra enfin se dire qu'il a grandi. Comme un enfant à la recherche de son vocabulaire, il a accompli le voyage qui le mène à la pleine maturité. Il a trente-six ans. Il peut désormais commencer à remplir ces trous que comportait cette lettre, dans laquelle il se proposait de donner des nouvelles de l'Afrique. Il peut désormais commencer à questionner l'Afrique, à l'écrire, plastiquement, telle qu'il la ressent et qu'il la vécue, une histoire à nulle autre pareille qui viendra apporter son chapitre au grand livre de l'humanité. L'artiste lui-même n'a pas manqué de mentionner ces différentes étapes qui l'ont conduit à son travail d'aujourd'hui. Ecoutons-le: "The hyperbolic imagery-laden Nigerian Pidgin, the Nok terracotta I saw first-hand in the Jos Museum and which to me embody some of the finest examples of authentic clay language, the solitary Akwanshi monoliths which make their evocative statements with organic restraint, *Uli*, that terse economical, space-animating and spontaneous painting tradition of the Igbo among whom I have lived for the past half-decade, the crop of very active contemporary artists and writers, to mention just a few, have continued to provide sources of inspiration, sustenance, influence and encouragement to me throughout these years."[5]

Pour un sculpteur africain, l'histoire n'est rien d'autre que la combinaison entre la tradition, la société et l'expérience personnelle. Celle d'El Anatsui se confond sans doute avec celle d'un matériau qu'il a appris à maîtriser, qu'il a su respecter dès son plus jeune âge, et qui enferme un savoir inaccessible à qui n'y a pas été initié: le bois. Parce que, nous dit-il, «Natural materials to me have more authenticity and substance than synthetic ones which seek to imitate anything, and have neither a culture of their own nor identity. » Par initiation, il ne faut pas entendre uniquement la cérémonie qui fait passer de l'enfance à l'âge d'homme, même si les deux phénomènes se confondent. Cette initiation représente l'histoire dont longtemps l'on a voulu croire l'Afrique privée. Parce que l'Afrique, disait-on, ne produisait aucune preuve tangible de son appartenance au monde civilisé. Mais ce qui jusqu'à il y a peu avait échappé au regard extérieur était cet ensemble de signes qui ne se livre pas au premier venu. Cette calligraphie dont la fonction était précise, comme *Uli* ou d'autres formes d'écriture au nombre desquelles je place la sculpture.

Quiconque veut se pencher sur l'histoire de l'Afrique et la connaître n'a qu'à se pencher sur sa statuaire. Quel que soit le pays où l'on se trouve sur le continent, l'on s'apercevra très rapidement que cette forme d'art n'existe que pour témoigner d'un monde, de rites et d'histoires particulières, avec une précision qu'aucune écriture, latine, arabe ou grecque ne saura égaler. Cette seule histoire que, il y a peu de temps encore, on appelait tradition. On a voulu figer la tradition, comme si elle avait été l'apanage, le signe distinctif des seuls pays du soit-disant Tiers-Monde. La tradition elle-même est devenue un concept ambigu. Tant d'ethnologues et d'anthropologues, les seuls

[5]El Anatsui, 'Sankofa,' op cit, p40. "Le Pidgin du Nigeria aux très nombreuses images hyperboliques, les terres cuites Nok que j'ai moi-même vues au Musée Jos et qui sont à compter à mon sens parmi les meilleurs exemples d'un langage authentique de l'argile, les monolithes solitaires Akwanshi quit profèrent leur déclarations évocatrices avec une retenue organique, la tradition des peintures *Uli* des Igbo — chez lesquels j'ai séjourné pendant ces cinq dernières années — peintures d'une spontanéité qui anime l'espace dans une économie de moyens, la production d'artistes et d'écrivains contemporains prolifiques, pour ne mentionner que quelques exemples, n'ont cessé de constituer pour moi des sources d'inspiration, une nourriture de l'esprit, une influence et un encouragement au fil des ans."

habilités jusqu'à il y a peu, à parler de la création africaine, nous ont laissés croire que le propre de l'Afrique était de reproduire dans son geste et sa pensée, une tradition immuable. Il ne pouvait y avoir d'art africain qui ne fût en étroite liaison avec la sacralité. L'Afrique était, dès lors, ce continent immobile voué à la pureté originelle. D'ailleurs, n'a-t-on pas, pour qualifier la statuaire africaine choisi le mot " primitif." Primitif pour dire quoi ? Pour dire que cet art- là est resté près des origines. Et, par voie de conséquence, ceux qui le produisaient. Mieux, qu'elle est enferrée dans l'origine, avec pour seules références les cérémonies rituelles et autres manifestations cultuelles. Pas de création donc, puisque cette production était avant tout fonctionnelle. Dans son livre, *Primitive Art in Civilized Places*, Sally Price démontre avec une rigueur documentée ce détournement qui a encore cours aujourd'hui, et dont on s'est servi comme un outil idéologique sans réelle base scientifique.

Qui d'entre nous, aux quatre coins du monde, peut prétendre échapper à la tradition? Car qu'est la tradition si ce n'est le conscient ou l'inconscient culturel d'un groupe donné? Le milieu à partir duquel on se propulse dans le monde? Le miroir à partir duquel on mesure l'altérité et la ressemblance? El Anatsui nous rappelait, avec des mots d'une justesse imparable, cette vérité intemporelle: si l'on considère que la vie est le sujet essentiel de la création artistique, alors l'on doit admettre également que cette vie, étroitement liée à la tradition et l'histoire, est immuable. La création est simplement une affaire de vision. Et seul le collage nous permet d'aller au-delà de ce qui a été, en nous faisant bénéficier d'un supplément de bagage et d'expérience.

Spiritualité et Contemporanéité

El Anatsui a fait partie de ces quelques artistes africains qui ont revendiqué leurs traditions et leur rapport à la sacralité. Il a compris qu'il eût été vain de prétendre ex nihilo, créer un monde nouveau. De vouloir, à l'image des Calder, Serra et autres sculpteurs occidentaux (desquels il convient tout de même de distinguer des exceptions comme l'Espagnol Jaume Plensa et le Français Nicolas Alquin) qu'Olu Oguibé mentionnait fort justement, prendre la place de Dieu. Le monde nouveau n'est rien d'autre que la traduction, dans une écriture contemporaine, d'un monde ancien. Une autre perspective, une autre façon de voir. Le déplacement qui commande nécessairement tout décalage temporel nous fait envisager les objets et les formes au-delà de leur fonction première. Exactement comme Picasso et le masque. Mais dès lors que l'on est investi, en plus de l'aspect strictement plastique et novateur, d'un savoir qui renvoie à son histoire, on est investi d'une force de création accrue, car le regard devient double. On décrypte soudain le sens à la fois par les yeux du corps et par ceux de l'esprit. Et les solutions plastiques que l'on envisage ne sont pas seulement ancrées dans la contemporanéité, mais elles font sens. Qu'importe que ce sens ne soit pas perceptible, immédiatement à tout un chacun. Il est sensible et rehausse l'œuvre d'art d'une dimension supérieure. Dans un monde où il était devenu de bon ton d'éviter toute référence passéiste en comprenant mal l'injonction de Rimbaud selon laquelle "il faut être résolument moderne. "Car la modernité ne se décrète pas, elle se vit. Et lorsque le sculpteur ghanéen dit qu'il ne comprend pas pourquoi un artiste se servirait d'éléments synthétiques pour arriver au même résultat avec des éléments naturels il énonce une position esthétique, philosophique et plastique qui constitue aujourd'hui, la seule véritable frontière entre les différentes formes d'art qui ont été produites dans cette seconde moitié du vingtième siècle. "There are artists using extreme exploratory processes effectively. But for every process you have a lot of people doing it unimaginatively, and a few who are doing something worth nothing. I have seen the work of some people using computers and other high-tech processes, and they are very exciting. I do not think that process is the beginning and end.

It is one of the components and, depending on how one handles it, it could make the difference between a creative mind and a technical hand."[6] Cette position, énoncée sans aucune espèce de vélléité polémique, constitue la seule véritable position révolutionnaire dans l'art d'aujourd'hui. Il est à noter, sans vouloir tomber dans le piège de l'ethnocentrisme facile, mais simplement comme une constat objectif, que cette révolution ne pouvait pas venir de l'Occident, trop empêtré dans un discours sur l'art qui est parvenu à occulter l'art lui-même. Et le grand vide des années 80 atteste, mieux que tout long développement, la panne que traverse l'inspiration de l'art international.

Depuis Duchamp, nous aurions dû commencer à nous poser des questions fondamentales sur la finalité de l'art dans la seconde moitié du vingtième siècle. J'ignore si ces questions furent posées de façon satisfaisante, mais ce qui reste, lorsque nous nous penchons sur l'évolution de la création de ces dernières années, indique clairement que la réponse n'a pas été trouvée. Et lorsque André Malraux nous annonçait que "le vingt-et-unième siècle serait spirituel ou ne serait pas," je me demande s'il avait une pleine conscience de la portée de son illumination. Et c'est bien là l'un des paradoxes les plus intéressants des temps que nous vivons que l'histoire exclusive qui avait été écrite par d'autres et pour d'autres ne puisse survivre que par l'apport de la périphérie. Car la *Périphérie* s'est mise à penser par elle-même et non plus uniquement par opposition ou mimétisme à l'égard du *Centre.*

Les limites de *la raison raisonnante* ayant été atteintes et dépassés, il est devenu évident que seule la raison *intuitive* pouvait nous sortir de l'impasse. Il n'est pas à douter que, à l'instar de tout processus révolutionnaire, il faille quelques années pour redéfinir cette nouvelle histoire qui ne se contenterait pas d'un universalisme réservé et décidé par l'Occident, mais d'un *pluriversalisme* planétaire dans lequel chacun apportera sa pierre. Est-ce vraiment un hasard si tout l'art moderne occidental, et par conséquent tout l'art contemporain occidental a connu son essor, son tournant fondateur avec la statuaire africaine et l'interprétation de Picasso et des cubistes? Il était clair dès lors que les sources d'inspiration devraient se trouver ailleurs.

Nous découvrons depuis quelques années que la séparation est impossible et que la tradition, quelle que soit l'œuvre ou l'artiste sur lesquels on se penche, est la permanence qui permet d'accéder à autre chose, qu'à défaut du terme modernité, trop connoté à l'histoire de l'art occidental, nous appellerons *nouveauté.* C'est la raison pour laquelle il est permis d'affirmer que le dialogue entre les artistes africains et le monde n'a jamais cessé. L'esclavage, la colonisation ont fonctionné comme autant de machines à broyer, à laver les cerveaux et à inscrire le doute comme élément premier des relations entre le colon et le colonisé. Il a fallu, dans une douloureuse psychanalyse, reprendre confiance et retrouver par soi-même et pour soi-même tous ces ensembles de signes et de sens desquels nous avons été coupés. Et une œuvre qui engloberait toute cette cosmogonie, qui rassemblerait l'ancien et le nouveau pour bâtir l'avenir deviendrait dès lors d'une indispensable évidence.

Il est capital d'inscrire tout artiste africain dans le cours d'une histoire qui certes prend pour point de départ le continent noir, mais ne s'arrête pas à ses seules frontières. Le piège de la contextualisation a été de toujours vouloir inscrire un artiste, pour peu qu'il fût issu de la Périphérie, dans un champ d'inspiration et de création spécifique. Limitant ainsi à sa seule ethnie et à son seul continent la portée de son œuvre. Or nous sommes tous conscients aujourd'hui que la création, la vraie, ne peut avoir de portée que planétaire. L'humanité n'est pas multiple. Elle est une et indivisible. Et El Anatsui nous l'a fait toucher du doigt dans une anecdote qui fût provoquée par l'une de ses performances en Allemagne, à Cuxhaven. Là-bas, s'était instauré un dialogue entre lui et une femme allemande qui retrouvait dans l'essence même du rituel auquel

[6]ibid, p41, "Il existe des artistes qui utilisent efficacement des procédés exploratoires extrêmes. Mais pour chacun de ces procédés, nombreux sont ceux qui le font sans imagination et quelques-uns réalisent des choses sans aucune valeur. J'ai vu les travaux de certains artistes qui recourent à l'ordinateur ou à d'autres procédés high-tech, et ils sont enthousiasmants. Je ne crois pas cependant que le procédé soit l'alpha et l'omega. Ce n'est que l'un des composants et c'est la façon dont on l'utilise quit fait toute la différence entre un esprit créatif et un coup de main technique."

elle venait d'assister une part d'elle-même. La tradition africaine est une tradition parmi d'autres qui fonctionne certes selon des codes spécifiques, mais à partir d'une mécanique qui demeure la même, quel que puisse être le coin de la planète dans lequel on a grandi. Il suffit de parcourir des recueils de contes issus du monde entier pour s'en persuader, si besoin était.

Les déités vaudous que l'on retrouve au Ghana, au Nigéria, au Bénin, à Cuba et au Brésil, sont les frères des dieux grecs de l'olympe et des dieux nordiques du Vallhalah. El Anatsui et ceux qui, comme lui, reconnaissent une immanence à la base de leur création ne font que rétablir la réalité de la fraternité qui nous lie les uns aux autres. En amplifiant ce qui nous ressemble plutôt que d'insister sur ce qui nous sépare et qui, finalement, est assez négligeable. Et c'est en remettant les choses dans leur vraie perspective que nous faisons œuvre d'historiens des temps à venir. La lecture historique du travail de El Anatsui est une lecture universelle, à partir du moment où elle s'inscrit dans un particularisme donné. L'homme ne saurait vivre en dehors du monde. Et l'œuvre d'art est comme la reproduction d'une cosmogonie très complexe dont la nature même serait la représentation du monde. Un monde fini et infini, proche et lointain, connu et inconnu. Un monde qui remet l'homme à sa véritable place, dans le temps et dans l'espace.

"Express new ideas in old wood. Mix time-furrowed
experience with buoyant smoothness; the concavity of old time with the convex posture of
new time.
New wood has poetry locked in it.
Old wood is poetry itself, time
Having worn off its prose
what do you do with pant singlet towel *buba* cloth?
You at least must have heard the background and
inside stories narrated by the people in assorted voices."[7]

[7]Extract from *Old and New,* a poem by El Anatsui quoted in Exhibition Catalogue, National Museum Lagos. Enugu: SNAAP Press, 1991."Exprime des idées neuves dans du vieux bois. Mêle l'expérience sillonnée par le temps à l'énergie flamboyante des textures lisses, les formes concaves du passé à la posture convexe d'une époque nouvelle.
Le bois jeune est un réceptacle de poésie.
Le bois vieux est la poésie elle-même, le temps
ayant usé sa prose
que fait-on de l'étoffe de nos vêtements?
Tu dois au moins avoir entendu le vieux fonds
d'histoires intimes que l'on narre dans un concert de voix."

Le titre des œuvres de El Anatsui, *Broken Chambers of Memory, At The Ancestors Conference (page p. 49), Writing Excerpts from Africa's History, Mahogany Force*, sa passion pour le bois et les matériaux naturels témoignent de cette volonté de fusionner avec les éléments, d'agir sur la nature comme un passeur, un sorcier illuminé qui aurait accès à des informations à côté desquelles nous passons tous les jours. La spiritualité n'est pas lourde et envahissante. Elle transparaît à travers les lignes fines, la verticalité de la sculpture ou la communauté retrouvée. Chacune de ses œuvres semble nous éclairer sur nous-même. Elles nous renvoient à notre grandeur et à notre petitesse. Elles nous sont, en un mot, indispensables, en nous révélant, par touches subtiles et lumineuses, quelques vérités de notre temps et de notre histoire. Nos histoires.

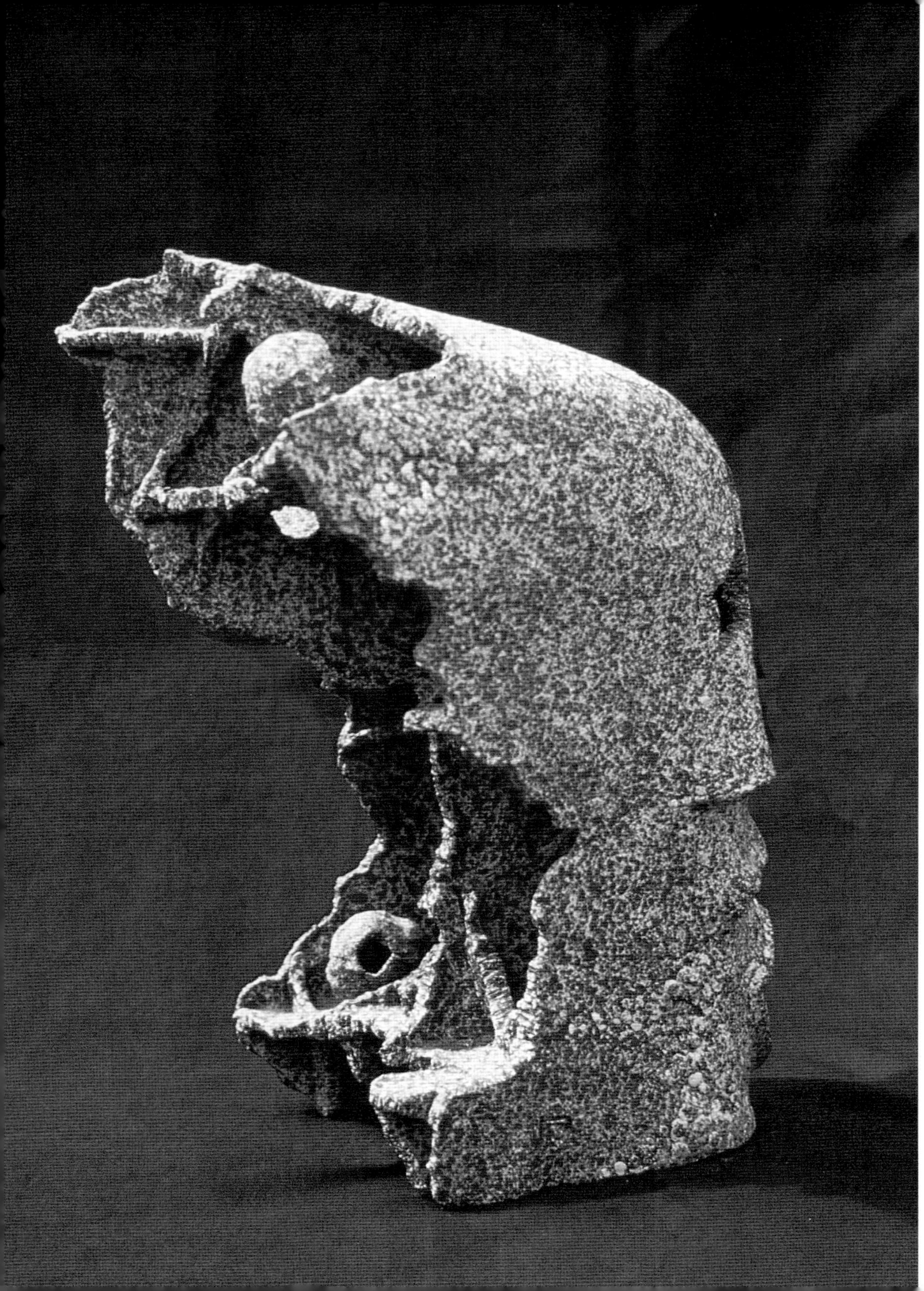

Chambers of Memory, 1977

ceramic-manganese body
height 40cm, width 29.3cm, depth 27cm

Photo: El Anatsui

E A PÉRI-WILLIS

Chambers of Memory

EL ANATSUI was born in Anyako, in 1944, in the Ewe-speaking area of southern Ghana. He studied sculpture and art education at the University of Science and Technology, Kumasi, and from 1969 lectured in the Art Education Department of the Specialist Training College (STC), now the University College of Education, at Winneba. Many of the first and second generations of modern Ghanaian sculptors, were trained in western sculptural traditions by European teachers, as were the painters, who were trained in oil painting techniques and used western representational styles to treat African subjects. In the years leading up to Ghanaian Independence in 1957, however, many artists began to reject these foreign influences.

Key figures in the history of modern Ghanaian art include: the sculptors, Oku Ampofo (b 1908) who worked in ebony and concrete; Vincent Akwete Kofi (b 1927) who worked mainly in wood; and the painter Kofi Antubam (b 1922).[1] The individual legacies of these early modern Ghanaian artists were not to influence Anatsui directly. Yet the circumstances that framed his development as a sculptor were contingent upon the increased awareness of the importance and value of indigenous art forms which those artists had done so much to promote. Antubam, a member of the Akan aristocracy, who wrote *Ghana's Heritage of Culture*, was the first to identify the potential for using Akan emblems in modern Ghanaian art. Kwame Nkrumah, the first President of Ghana, employed Antubam as his

[1]Fosu, Kojo, *20th Century Art of Africa* (Zaria, Nigeria: Gaskiya Corporation Ltd,1986), p14-18, 156-159.

Elizabeth Péri-Willis, born in England, completed a degree in Painting at Camberwell Art School, London in 1982 and painted for some time before a voyage to the Sudan elicited an interest in African art. In 1985, as a Commonwealth Scholar, she went to the University of Nigeria, Nsukka, to do a Masters Degree in Painting where she first met El Anatsui. Her own painting has been much influenced by her research on the exclusively women's art of mural and body painting known as uli. *Between 1987 and 1989 she taught painting at the University of Maiduguri, in northern Nigeria, after which she returned to England where she completed her PhD in African Art History at the School of Oriental and African Studies, University of London, in 1997, with a dissertation on twentieth-century developments in art in southeastern Nigeria. She has exhibited her work both in Nigeria and the UK, and is the author of numerous articles on the traditions of* uli *painting. She is currently involved in research into modern Ghanaian art.*

cultural advisor, and in the years prior to and immediately following Independence, Antubam produced many works that served to promote visual identities encouraging a new national awareness in Ghana. Antubam also incorporated Akan *adinkra* patterns[2] into the designs for the mace of the new Parliament, as well as many other State emblems.

Vincent Akwete Kofi was inspired by the organic shapes of natural forms and would sometimes retain the natural splits found in wood to represent aspects of the anatomy of his figural sculptures. He also drew upon the artistic traditions of Ghana's past. In *Awakening Africa* and *Birth of Ghana* the heads of his sculpted figures resemble the style found in Akan *akuaba* fertility figures.[3] In 1965, the year after Antubam's death, while still a first year student at Kumasi, Anatsui was selected to work on heraldic sculptures for the Organisation of African Unity (OAU) Conference in Accra.[4] This enabled him to experience first hand how the modern artist could play a significant role in the development of a national identity and to see how art could be employed in developing the aspirations and celebrating the achievements of the whole African continent.

El Anatsui's early artistic development was thus much affected by various elements operating in the ambient art world as he was completing university education and, again, during his formative years as an artist in Winneba. Anatsui continued to feel that the training he received at Kumasi, based largely on western art practice, was inadequate, if not entirely alienating, and he began the search to develop an artistic perspective more in keeping with his own particular sympathies. During his final year he began to visit the National Cultural Centre at Kumasi almost every weekend. There he watched weavers, potters, *adinkra* cloth printers and carvers at work, and saw how many of these craftsmen still used 'traditional' motifs in their works, or listened to local musicians, savouring the harmonious medley of sounds they made as they performed. Anatsui thus became exposed to the full range of indigenous arts and crafts, which he had been unable to explore during his years of formal art training. These visits and the insights they afforded into the indigenous traditions of design were crucial influences that enabled him to develop in new, more personally sympathetic, artistic directions.

On taking up the post of art lecturer at the STC Winneba (his arrival coinciding with Vincent Akwete Kofi's departure for Kumasi), Anatsui was able to explore for the first time ways in which local forms, such as the Akan *adinkra* emblems could be used as design resources to be incorporated into his own sculptures. Here, during the early 1970s Anatsui was associated with a group of artists who held annual exhibitions, both at Winneba and Accra, under the name of Tekarts. Amongst the many members of what Anatsui describes as 'the art family at Winneba,' were the painters Desmond Fiadjoe, Phillip Amonoo, David Adotia, Seth Zoyinral, the graphic artist Robert Tettey, the textile artists Edith Agbenaza and Hope Gamor and the ceramicist Richard Ekem.[5]

One particular *adinkra* emblem represents the *sankofa* bird, a bird known for its habit of frequently looking backwards. The idea associated with this design is that one should not be afraid to look behind and learn from past mistakes.[6] *Sankofa* means 'return' and 'retrieve' in the Twi language or, translated into more idiomatic language, 'Go back and pick.'[7] In Ghana, during the 1950s and 1960s, visual and non-visual artists alike used *sankofa* as a rallying call to describe their position on the consuming question of foreign stylistic influences versus local traditions. Anatsui describes *sankofa* as:

> "a reaction to a conscious and forcible attempt to denigrate a people's culture and replace it with an extraneous one…it recognised also that there are always elements of an invading culture which stay behind; you cannot obliterate it completely because every culture has its positive aspects. Thus the essence [of *sankofa*] was neither a wholesale return to the past nor

[2] *adinkra* patterns are mostly non-figurative emblems which are "printed on to an otherwise plain textile using stamps cut from pieces of calabash with a glutinous black pigment. The emblems each have specific proverbial connotations but are not used with any kind of syntactic intention, rather as a more general presentation of moral principle." J Picton, *The Art of African Textiles: Technology, Tradition and Lurex*, London: Lund Humphries Publishers, 1995, p21. J Picton, and J Mack, *African Textiles* (London: British Museum Publications Ltd, second edition, 1989), p165. *Adinkra* means 'saying farewell' and in the past *Adinkra* cloth was worn mainly at funerals.

[3] Fosu, Kojo, *20th Century Art of Africa*, op cit, 1986, p159, 160.

[4] Anatsui made coats of arms in terracotta for Ghana, Uganda, Tunisia and Zambia.

[5] Anatsui, E, personal communication with the author, April, 1998.

[6] Picton, J, *The Art of African Textiles*, 1995, op cit, p21.

[7] From Olu Oguibe's interview with El Anatsui, 'Sankofa: Go Back an' Pick. Three Studio Notes and a Conversation,' *Third Text: Third World Perspectives on Contemporary Art and Culture*, No 23, Summer 1993, p50, London: Kala Press.

a total exclusion of external influence. The thrust was inward orientation and selectivity."[8]

[8]ibid, p51.

In the early years of his career (1969-1975) Anatsui made reference to Ewe pottery forms, to the colours and patterns of both Ewe and Asante strip weaving and to *adinkra* motifs. The experience of studying pottery and textile forms enabled him to begin to think more deeply about their meaning and resonance in social and historical terms in his own locality and in other parts of Africa. In 1970 Anatsui began a series of wooden plaques which were inspired by the circular wooden trays on which Winneba market women displayed their goods. He contacted the carvers who made the trays, and commissioned both standard designs and more unusual formats to suit his own purposes.[9] The largest wooden plaques were some 75 centimetres (about 29 inches) in diameter with a raised rim about 6.5 centimetres (two and a half inches) wide around the circumference. The central circular shape had a slightly convex surface. Anatsui drew motifs or patterns on the rim thereby providing a frame for the designs and images of the raised central area. These included *adinkra* emblems signifying, for example, *Hope, Wisdom, Versatility*, and *Peace*. He then scorched the patterns he had traced by applying heated rods or knives, borrowing from the indigenous techniques of local artisans who used this method to decorate calabashes or the bows of canoes. In at least one circular wall plaque the central portion contains schematised representations of footprints, signifying people taking different routes from one place to arrive together at another place in a new land. Entitled *Their Fateful Journey Nowhere* (1975),[10] this is one of Anatsui's earliest sculptures to take as its subject migrations and the mass movement of peoples, a subject which has continued to exercise him for close to three decades. Thin perpendicular lines painted red, yellow, white and orange, reminiscent of the colour harmonies of Kente cloth, divide the rimmed section into irregular sections which contain scorched patterns, and small, golden, lozenge shapes of thinly-beaten copper. The metal is evocative of gold not only from the Akan gold fields, but also from mines elsewhere, the search for which might have been a likely cause of so many "fateful" journeys. The idea of taking a simple domestic object and recreating it, by giving it a new artistic form, is a strategy that Anatsui has repeated and developed at different stages of his career.

[9]Ottenberg, S, *New Traditions from Nigeria: Seven Artists of the Nsukka Group* (Washington, DC: Smithsonian Institution Press in association with the National Museum of African Art, 1997), p157.

[10]This work is in the private collection of Sandor Péri.

Anatsui left Ghana in 1975 to join the Department of Fine and Applied Art at the University of Nigeria, Nsukka. There he met the artist Uche Okeke, who as an art student in 1958, two years before Nigerian Independence, had led a group of artists to form the Zaria Art Society and developed the idea of 'Natural Synthesis.' The principle of 'Natural Synthesis' was born from the desire to develop a modern Nigerian art that would blend indigenous art forms with the best of western methods and materials.[11] The adoption of western techniques, other external influences and the use of new materials were accepted as logical and quite consistent with local aspirations for independent progress and modernisation. In reality, these modern Nigerian artists were simply continuing the traditions of African art in which exchanges have always taken place between Africa, Europe and other continents, and African artists and artisans developed their own traditions of practice by being awake to the possibilities offered by new materials, images and technologies.[12] The idea of 'Natural Synthesis,' which Okeke reintroduced when he joined the University of Nigeria at Nsukka in 1972, two years after the end of the Nigerian Civil War, shared so much common ground with the Ghanaian *sankofa* syndrome that Anatsui found it relevant to his own methods of working when he arrived in Nsukka shortly thereafter.

[11]Willis, E A, *Uli Painting and Identity: Twentieth Century Developments in Art in the Igbo-speaking Region of Nigeria*, University of London, PhD thesis, 1997, pp237-239.

[12]Picton, J, *The Art of African Textiles, 1995,* op cit, p12.

Many of the artists working at Nsukka followed Okeke's lead in becoming interested in the *uli* idiom, a corpus of motifs used mainly by the Igbo-speaking people in body decorations and wall painting, and began to incorporate both the designs themselves and certain formal qualities of the system into their art-works.[13] Okeke defines *uli* as a system of drawing, but the highly schematised motifs signified everyday objects, plants and animals, as well as conceptual notions such as the actions of cutting and bending. Together with his new colleagues Anatsui explored the possibilities offered by this local art form. He also became interested in *nsibidi*, a secret code of emblems used by the Leopard (Ekpé) secret society in southeastern Nigeria. In conjunction with his earlier interest in *adinkra* emblems, the study of *uli* design strategies and motifs and of *nsibidi* elements provided Anatsui with alternative frames of reference by which to view the world, enabling him, as he puts it, to:

> "conceive of things not in their vulgar physique…to delve deeper below the surface of events, objects, people and experiences, in an attempt to seek visual meanings and truths; to distil essences, to decipher symbolic contents."[14]

Of the many sculptural traditions in Nigeria, ranging from the delicate and elaborate Igbo-Ukwu bronzes to the highly naturalistic terracotta portraits from Ile-Ife, Anatsui was drawn to two in particular. He admired the simple stone monoliths from Akwanshi, which were sparingly engraved with geometric shapes, and Nok terracotta sculptures of which the earliest date back to the second half of the first millennium BC. Nok sculptures represent human figures, the heads having quite distinctive features. The eyes are usually given prominence with the pupils represented by deep holes pierced into the clay while the stylised eyebrows are indicated by shallow triangles or semi-circles scored in the clay. The nose and the mouth are also represented by deep incisions. Surface details such as the hair, beads, necklaces and bracelets were sculpted by scoring, grooving, combing and stamping or by making roulette impressions.[15] The influence of the stylised facial characteristics of the ancient Nok figures can be seen in evidence in many of Anatsui's wood sculptures. Rather than incising and scoring the wet clay, however, Anatsui has used modern power tools to make similar cuts and scored marks when rendering the hair and features of the figures that ornament his wooden wall hangings and standing screens. The incorporation of such indigenous elements into his sculpture, which gives Anatsui's works their particular cultural dispositions, is only one of the levels at which his works function. Through such references he can explore and render his own response to African history. Anatsui believes that historical accounts about the continent of Africa written by outsiders have done much to distort the real histories of its peoples. Questions relating to origins and historiography are problematic in those parts of sub-Saharan Africa that are considered by outsiders never to have developed systems of writing, and, where there is a perceived lack of written texts the history of those places has suffered from neglect. In response to such facile assumptions Anatsui has spent much time researching the various writing systems that developed in Africa, the codes and ideographs, as well as the numerous systems of visual design. Anatsui uses such sign languages and visual systems to try to enter the minds of the people that used them, suggesting that the historical gaps can be bridged by an act of the creative imagination. Some gaps, however, will always persist, and in *The Face of Africa's History* (1988) and *Patches of History III* (1993, colour plate, p43) these are represented by large areas of scorched wood.

Anatsui's position within what has come to be known as the Nsukka Group of artists has, since 1976, brought him opportunities to exhibit with them both in Nigeria and overseas. However, Anatsui's sculptural output has been so prolific, and his creative energy so focused that by means of both solo and international group exhibitions he has also established a personal reputation as a major

[13] Ottenberg, S, *New Traditions from Nigeria,* 1997, op cit.

[14] Anatsui, E, *Pieces of Wood* (Enugu, Nigeria: SNAAP Press, 1987). Exhibition catalogue. p10

[15] Fagg, B, *Nok Terracottas* (London: Ethnographica, second edition, 1990), p24-26.

force in contemporary sculpture both at home in Nigeria and also abroad. In 1990 Anatsui exhibited at the Studio Museum, Harlem, New York, and was one of five artists chosen to represent Africa for the first time at the 44th Venice Biennale. His work was shown at the 5th Havana Biennale in 1994: and in 1995, at the first Johannesburg Biennale and *Configura 2*, Erfurt, Germany. In the same year a series of art exhibitions and associated events took place throughout the UK under the umbrella title of *africa95*. During this time Anatsui held his first individual exhibition in London at the October Gallery and was also represented in the *Seven Stories about Modern Art in Africa* exhibition at the Whitechapel Art Gallery, London. In 1997 he was one of seven artists from the Nsukka Group to exhibit in *The Poetics of Line* exhibition at the Gallery of Modern African Art at the National Museum of African Art, Washington, DC. He has also participated in workshops, artists' exchange programmes and residencies in the UK, the USA, Denmark, Germany, Italy and Namibia.

Despite the increasing calls of overseas engagements Anatsui has nevertheless kept Nsukka as his base. He appreciates the contrast between the modern university campus, the urban developments in the town of Nsukka, and the natural environment of rural farms and homesteads in villages all within a few miles of the campus. It is in these surrounding villages that Anatsui finds new materials for his sculpture, as well as subjects for his work, for example *Old Lace and Television Aerials*, *Queue for Plastic Goods* (1985) and *Women's Club* (1986). Anatsui has acknowledged the fruitful character of these natural surroundings, the importance of the contact he maintains with artists and writers within the university as well as with villagers and carvers with whom he spends time looking for wood (both new and old) with which to begin new works.[16] Between these two contiguous worlds he is assured of access to the wide range of indigenous Nigerian art forms. Overshadowing all else, however, is the unstable political situation that has so affected the lives of all within and outside of the University community.

On his journeys overseas to participate in workshops and residencies, Anatsui says he enjoys the feelings of heightened concentration and focus that occur. Distance from his usual workplace offers him, he thinks, an atmosphere enabling him to reflect upon and sift through the complex array of stimuli provided by home. "It is like drawing a long line. You need distance to assess its course from time to time."[17] It has been during such periods of "distancing" that Anatsui has experienced important watersheds in his career. He cites excursions to Cummington, Massachusetts, USA (1980),[18] Redruth, UK (1985),[19] Manaus, Brazil (1992),[20] Copenhagen, and Helsingør in (1996)[21] as being major influences on his artistic development. It was in Cummington that he began to work with the chainsaw as a sculptural tool, using it to carve planks of wood that then could be formed into standing screens or wall hangings, and in Redruth that he consolidated and changed aspects of his ceramic images. In Manaus (*Arte Amazonas*), Anatsui produced *Erosion* which was a major statement employing a range of vocabularies, both technical and visual, that he had built up over a decade. In *Container 96*, an exhibition in Copenhagen, each artist was given a transport container as an exhibition space. This presented him with new possibilities for the exhibition of his chainsaw explorations. At Helsingør, work produced for the exhibition *Images of Africa* points to a major breakthrough in his use and treatment of found/ready-made objects, which had begun with the use of market-women's trays in 1970 and continued during the 1980s with the re-appropriation of disused mortars and house posts.[22]

Anatsui's first experience of what he refers to as "distancing" — migrating, moving away from the known — occurred when he left Ghana for Nigeria. This move appears to have been the catalyst for a change in materials. Between 1976 and 1982 and for a further period in 1985 Anatsui worked in clay. While making references to the Ewe pottery forms and the texture and nuances of colour of the Nok

[16] Anatsui, E, personal communication with the author, April, 1998.

[17] ibid.

[18] Anatsui was artist-in-residence at the Community of Arts, Cummington, Mass., USA.

[19] Anatsui was visiting artist at Cornwall College, Redruth, UK, 1985. The works he produced were exhibited in 1987 in *Venovize: Ceramic Sculptures*, a solo exhibition of ceramic sculpture at the Faculty of Art and Design, Cornwall College. My thanks to Janet Stanley, Librarian at the National Museum of African Art, Smithsonian Institution, Washington, D.C., for providing that exhibition catalogue and other texts on El Anatsui.

[20] *The Arte Amazonas* environmental sculpture project was connected with the Earth Summit meeting in Rio de Janeiro, 1992.Works produced by artists invited for the project were exhibited at the Museum of Modern Art, Rio de Janeiro.

[21] Anatsui took part in an international artists' workshop in Helsingør where he made work for the exhibition *Images of Africa*, Torpedohallen, Copenhagen.

[22] Anatsui, E, personal communication with the author, April, 1998.

terracottas, which he had seen at the Jos Museum in Nigeria, he also experimented with modern ceramic techniques. Nsukka had a modern, high temperature kiln which enabled Anatsui to make a stoneware type of pottery. He used local clay, manganese tailings from Ghana, pieces of glass and potsherds, which he mixed together.[23]

His first exhibition of ceramics in Nsukka, in 1979, *Broken Pots*, included the work *Chambers of Memory*, Anatsui's only ceramic work to have a stylistic resemblance to Nok sculpture, though this appears to have been achieved by accident. Ottenberg has described how Anatsui draped a clay slab on wood, which hardened to become strangely elongated, but looking like a Nok head.[24] However, at the back of the head, where the skull should be, there are irregular chambers containing nothing. In 1982, Anatsui wrote, in the introduction to his second ceramic exhibition at the Goethe Institute, Lagos:

> "All of Africa is undergoing a period of turmoil. There is despondence, despair, bewilderment and frustration all over. It is to this predicament that my attempt in these works to use decadence and destruction as elements of creation and reconstruction addresses a message. I hasten however to reiterate that regeneration and growth are not automatically consequent upon break-down. Conscious effort and intact chambers of memory to provide that grog of experience which strengthens the new form, are requisites."[25]

Other works in the *Broken Pots* series also allude to the possibility of regeneration. Anatsui made two types of broken pot. In the first, he made, fired and then broke a perfectly formed pot, leaving a container with jagged edges like a broken eggshell. These works may carry associations with the use of broken pots in the villages where they would be crushed, mixed with clay and reused to make new pots, or given a new function entirely, such as clay discs to make up a bracelet, or used as a small dish or oil-lamp.[26] In the second type of pot Anatsui made separate pieces which were then put together and fired. In these pots there would be holes, and crevices, and the surface would gain a patched appearance as the bits of pottery used were imprinted with various patterns and were of differing textures and hues. Thus, patching, mending, and making good are other forms of regenerative recycling and renewal.

Sculpture from New Wood, 1979-Present

At the end of the 1970s Anatsui resumed woodcarving. At this time his tools were limited to hammers, chisels and the blowtorch. However, a residency in 1980 at an artists' community in Cummington, Massachusetts, USA, introduced Anatsui to the potential of using a chainsaw in an innovative way. He had previously only used a chainsaw on excursions into the forests to choose wood or to cut large logs. In this new environment, a mixture of enabling factors — the size of his studio, its quiet serenity away from the hub of the colony — provided circumstances in which he began to imagine new possibilities for the chainsaw as a modern drawing tool.[27] Wall hangings and standing screens composed of interchangeable, vertical planks of wood became a characteristic feature of Anatsui's work from 1982 to the late 1980s.

A number of factors contributed to his decision to use vertical, hanging planks. Firstly, he felt that the format would allow him to work with the chainsaw in ways that he wanted to explore further. Secondly, such an arrangement of two-dimensional wooden planks was not unfamiliar to him. Wood carvers from the Awka area in southeastern Nigeria, for example, made doors, flanked by a series of side panels. These carvers, renowned for their expertise in the chip-carving technique, carved diagonal parallel lines, both straight and curved, as well as motifs, which were

[23] Ottenberg, S, *New Traditions from Nigeria*, op cit, p159-163.

[24] ibid., p162.

[25] Anatsui, E, extract from studio notes, 'Broken Pots: Chambers of Memory,' *Third Text*, 1993, p39.

[26] Foreword to brochure, *Broken Pots*, 1979, British Council, Enugu and Institute of African Studies, University of Nigeria, Nsukka, Nigeria.

[27] Anatsui, E, *Pieces of Wood*, exhibition catalogue, Enugu, Nigeria: SNAAP Press, 1987, pp9, 10.

[28] Picton, J, *The Art of African Textiles*, op cit, p20.

part of the *uli* painter's repertoire, onto the doors and surrounding panels. Finally, Anatsui also made an association between the adjacent, vertical, hanging strips of timber and the narrow-strip weaving techniques of the Ewe and Asante. The logic of this narrow-strip format enables the bold juxtaposing of patterns in the sewing together, edge to edge, of individual strips.[28] The historical implications of the making, development, and trading of cloth in Africa, together with its multiple uses and social connotations have always given textiles a special relevance for Anatsui. In the vertical wall hangings and standing screens Anatsui uses many of the simple geometric elements such as draughts, dots and triangles from his design sources, which include a wide range of woven and printed textiles, as can be seen, for example, in *City Against an Ancient Monument* (1991). He translates these designs into raised relief by using the chainsaw to cut out the large segments, heavy lines, angles and curvilinear shapes, before relying on other power-tools such as routers and gouges, more suitable to the engraving of the details and finer lines. The negative and positive areas of pattern are distinguished by using an acetylene torch to burn and blacken the wood. Anatsui also occasionally uses flashes of red, blue, green and yellow tempera paint. These small areas of saturated colour provide a vivid contrast both to the scorched areas and to the subtle gradations of the natural colour and grain of the wood. Parts of the panel might be scorched or cut so deeply as to pierce the wood, as in *Remnant of Grandma's Cloth* (1991, colour plate, p45). In this and in many similar works the edges of the panels are dramatically serrated.

Erosion (colour plate, p51), Anatsui's largest single sculpture to date was created during the *Arte Amazonas* artists' workshop prior to the Earth Summit meeting in Rio de Janeiro, Brazil in 1992. This monumental work expresses Anatsui's concerns about the erosion of cultures. Presented with the raw materials, the space and the machinery required to manipulate the nearly 4.5 metre-high tree-trunk from which this prodigious work was made, Anatsui decided to sculpt in the round. A previous exhibition of work in the round, entitled *Old and New*, which included *Wonder Masquerade* (colour plate, p54), had taken place in 1991 at the National Museum in Lagos. *Erosion* can be seen as the culmination of over eleven years of work with chainsaw, power tools, and pyrographic techniques and combines a mastery of those different disciplines with a broad knowledge of indigenous African writing and visual systems. The pillar of the trunk is cut away in a rising spiral of stepped segments, the discarded remnants of which litter the base of the work. On what remains of the column's outer surface are finely detailed patterns, scripts, ideograms and other pictographic elements. From certain perspectives the effects of the erosion seem little more than surface deep, but rounding the shaft, other angles show the destruction that has been wrought upon the pillar which seems almost ready to come crashing down. Like a cartographer, he has mapped on the surface contour lines, rivers and the anonymous glyphs of past civilisations. Indigenous societies still bearing an individuality, a cultural identity, are represented by their characteristic symbols, such as *adinkra* patterns, and *nsibidi* motifs. Where human figures are carved fleeing across the ravaged surface one senses whole peoples in migration, displaced from the safety of their cultural centres.

In *Leopard Cloth* (1995, colour plate, p55) Anatsui returns to the vertical wall-hanging form using several hardwoods: mansonia, camwood, opepe, and oyili oji. Compared to *Erosion*, *Leopard Cloth* is both restrained and austere, composed of four wooden slats irregularly divided into three horizontal bands of pattern. The upper part contains a continuous, seamless pattern of irregular small squares divided into two triangles. One triangular shape being cut away forces the other into high relief. Negative areas are scorched, contrasting with the subtle colouration of the natural surface of the wood. Small repetitive circular motifs containing even smaller circles are branded across the narrow band of the lowest section, while in between the circles and triangles, an expanse of roughly drawn, scorched lines represent figures in motion. The title *Leopard Cloth* is a reference to the cloth worn by initiates of the Leopard secret society, known as *ukara* cloth. Numerous other *nsibidi* designs appear within a grid of rectangles in *ukara* cloth (although circles do not). The repeated triangular patterns are an important identifying motif for the Leopard Society, representing the claws of a leopard. Anatsui limits himself to triangular patterns and to circles. He has said the circles are a personal emblematic shorthand that he associates with the leopard, [29] but they also recall the King of Adinkra motif, a series of concentric circles, which Anatsui has described elsewhere as a visually powerful motif.[30] Very similar representations of leopard's spots are seen on the naturalistic brass sculptures of leopards made for the King of Benin in southwestern Nigeria, in the sixteenth century.

[29]Anatsui, E, personal communication with the author, April, 1998.

[30]'West Africa: Art and Identities,' Nick Levinson and Catherine King, BBC Open University, London 1998.

The simple geometric patterns preferred by Anatsui, such as triangles and circles, are found in traditions of art, past and present, throughout the world, and may signify different things in different places. There could, therefore, be two broad responses to *Leopard Cloth.* The first from an audience aware of the Leopard Society's emblems; that the leopard has associations of power and status; and that certain African cloths are a means of identification, and the second from those able to appreciate its formal and schematic qualities in relation to the works of artists from different traditions. Anatsui is as familiar with the geometric, optical experiments of Bridget Riley as he is with the patterns and textures of West Africa. That some visual similarities in certain forms and arrangements of patterns (although these similarities may only be superficial) can be construed between Anatsui's art and works emerging from contemporary western traditions, has been identified by the curator of a joint exhibition of works by Anatsui and Sol LeWitt (Skoto Gallery, New York in July, 1996). These similarities were described by one reviewer as both striking and surprising, given that "Sol LeWitt's work emerges from minimalism and conceptual art and Anatsui's sculptures are steeped in African culture and are rich with historical references, linguistically based ideograms and decorative designs embedded with specific political and spiritual meanings."[31]

[31]Holland Cotter reviews the joint exhibition by El Anatsui and Sol LeWitt at the Skoto Gallery in *The New York Times*, July 5, 1996.

Perhaps more convincing and fundamental relationships are to be found between Anatsui's work and those contemporary western artists who make sculpture from natural, organic materials or find works already sculpted by nature; Andy Goldsworthy, Anya Gallaccio and Andrew Long come to mind. Anatsui has expressed his admiration for three western artists, Anthony Gormley, Marina Abramovic and Helen Escobedo because of their approaches to and use of natural materials. He featured with Gormley and Abramovic at the *Arte Amazonas* project, and with Escobedo at *Configura II.* Each has worked in wood and clay and produced sculptures that celebrate the presence and integrity of these materials.[32]

[32]Anatsui, E, personal communication with the author, April, 1998.

Old wood: Mortars, house posts and driftwood

> New wood has poetry locked in it
> Old wood is poetry itself, time
> having worn off its prose.[33]

In the late 1980s Anatsui began to collect disused mortars and house posts from villages close to Nsukka. Mortars, some up to ten foot long, were laid horizontally on the ground and used for pounding and extracting palm oil from palm kernels. Over time the pounding weakened the hollowed out tree trunk until it was of no further use and so was discarded. By standing the mortars up on one end Anatsui saw a way to transform dramatically these redundant forms. The first old mortar work, *Bright Underwear of a Fallen God,* is dated 1988. Using discarded objects to create something new is for Anatsui a metaphor for historical processes. Before working on the mortars Anatsui subjected them to a rite of passage using the low burrow-shaped hills (inselbergs) of the Nsukka area; hills which have

[33]Anatsui, E, in 'Artist's Studio Notes' in the catalogue for *Old and New: An Exhibition of Sculptures in Assorted Wood*, Lagos National Museum, 1991, p7.

inspired painters from the Nsukka group such as Obiora Udechukwu and Chike Aniakor, and poets Okogbule Wonodi and Ada Udechukwu. Anatsui used the hill-side as part of the creative process to make new forms from old:

"The decision was finally taken. Today we took these old mortars up the little hill and rolled them down. Old and weak portions retired from the main blocks after this ordeal, which is part of the process of selecting the viable wood as well as reshaping the original forms."[34] From the reshaped forms Anatsui sculpted a series of figures with titles such as *Spear Bearer* (1991) and *Tapper* (1995, *colour plate, p50*).

[34]ibid.

Anatsui also reshaped house posts that he had found and taken from derelict houses to create a series of works on the theme of ancestors. When an earthen house became dilapidated, the house-posts alone, being made of the hard wood okpeye, could be used again in a new building. Some house-posts supported homesteads for generations. As objects they were, therefore, appropriate metaphors for 'ancestor' figures.[35] In *The Ancestors Converged Again* (1995) and *At the Ancestors' Conference* (1995,*(colour plates, pp46, 47, 49*) Anatsui hangs individual posts side by side on a wall. He exploits their ready-made physical qualities by turning the stakes into figures, with the upside-down forked ends becoming the ancestors' legs. He saws or cuts horizontal and vertical bands on their torsos which he paints with yellow, red, blue and white stripes, and represents facial features in a highly schematised way.

[35]In Nigeria and Ghana second funerals are required before the deceased can proceed to the ancestor's sphere. At these events, great crowds gather to remember and celebrate the deceased. It is an extravagant affair, sometimes requiring years to amass the resources needed for it. Under certain conditions, the ancestor may be urged to come back to the world in another's body. El Anatsui has given his interpretation of *At the Ancestor's Conference:* "Normally our revered ancestors are at peace in their final resting places and are not easily aroused. It must therefore be very grim circumstances which will have them converge at a conference." This extract is from 'The Modern African Artist as Rebel: A Personal Perspective,' a paper presented by Anatsui at the University of Iowa, 1987.

Origins, Movement, Migrations

The Ewe have a history of movement and migration, and a number of Anatsui's wall hangings are about past journeys, some forced, some voluntary. Anatsui has represented large groups on the move since his first work on the subject in 1975, which shares the title given to a recent installation work *On Their Fateful Journey Nowhere* (1995). The installation may signify a family or clan, or a larger linguistic or territorial group. Whatever the interpretation, the figures appear passive, lacking control over their destiny. Many of Anatsui's groups seem to be in this state, as the titles of some works suggest: *They made it happen, watched it happen but now with dishevelled hair, wonder what happened* (1986), and *The elements threatened immediately above while we still milled around in a mass of complacency* (1989).

The African slave trade resulted in the forced removal of millions of people from the continent. Invited to create a work for the *Images of Africa Festival* in Helsingør, Denmark in 1996, Anatsui created an installation entitled *Akua's Surviving Children (colour plate, pp38-39)* which he considers to be a major development in his treatment of the found object. *Akua's Surviving Children* represents a clan of survivors from the Danish slave trade, which operated between Ghana, formerly the Gold Coast, and the Danish West Indies. The *Akua-ba* (Akua's child) is the name given to a Ghanaian fertility symbol. While walking on the beach at Hellebæk, in northern Denmark, he saw a log that had been washed up on the shore, which was weathered and shaped by the action of the sea, and had a rusty iron stake at one end. He stood the log up on one end (as he had done with the worn out mortars), and made a correlation between the washed up member and the victims of slavery, who had been "Torn from their land source into wild, hostile sea, tossed about, eventually returning to land with experiences of their ordeal."[36] The next day he found two more logs of driftwood washed up near the first. But as the slave trade dealt with vast numbers of people, many such logs would be needed to complete the metaphor. In the following days he walked many kilometres by the sea shore salvaging more and more logs until he had around thirty. Anatsui's workplace at Helsingør was a renovated iron forge, where, in the past, blacksmiths had made Dane guns used by the slave traders, some of which were sold on to Africans.

[36]Anatsui, E, unpublished notes on *Akua's Surviving Children*, 1996.

At this forge he carried out a ritual of restitution and cleansing by scorching some of the smaller logs that were later to become the heads of Akua's children: "Burning is a cleansing ritual still in use in parts of my society…On another level, having been exposed to the elements of water and wind, fire probably remained…to complete the experience of the cycle of wood."[37] Each head was fixed to the log body by nails which had been made on the forge. The current direction of Anatsui's sculpture seems to be moving away from carving and painting and towards a more sensitive appreciation of the natural grain and pattern of the wood of the found object.

[37]Ibid.

Movement and migration within the continent is still occurring. Some Africans seek refuge or travel outside the continent. These people are represented in *Visa Queue* (1992, colour plate, p12) as indistinguishable aliens. The scale and similarity of the figures and the technique of burning the figures at their edges produces an image that looks blurred and hazy. The people in line are seen to be 'out of focus,' indistinct and lacking individuality. Underlying this work is a sense of fatality; the figures have no environmental context and display no clues as to their identity or history. Yet this is the reality of displaced persons, political refugees, and others who are travelling towards inhospitable places.

Uli, Adinkra, Nsibidi

Anatsui does not simply copy individual *uli* motifs or *adinkra* or *nsibidi* motifs although he gives his own interpretation of some, such as leopard's paw, or the *nsibidi* sign for married love, which is two curved lines, or the *adinkra* emblem for versatility which consists of a series of short vertical and horizontal lines. In some works like *Earth-Moon Connexions* (1993, colour plate, p42) and *Remnant of Grandma's Cloth* (1995, colour plate, p45), Anatsui contrasts 'active areas' with negative space, recalling the spatial organisation of some *uli* designs, but the basic forms in the 'active area' are reminiscent of Ghanaian narrow strip weaving. Anatsui wants to understand different aesthetic motivations and vocabularies and, for him, learning about the signs of a people is a way towards understanding their culture. For example, he began to understand that *uli* designers might represent a plant or an animal by emphasising one important quality or aspect only. Anatsui used that strategy: deciding what is the most important identifying mark for the subject and using that as the focus of his work. In *Tapper* (1995, colour plate, p50), the clue to the figure's identity as a palm-wine tapper is the hoop slung over one shoulder. It is with such a hoop made of raffia palm that the tapper shimmies up the palm tree to tap the wine. The process of simplifying an object or figure to some essential aspect has been employed in Anatsui's more recent works such as *Akua's Surviving Children* (1996) and *On Their Fateful Journey Nowhere* (1996, colour plate, pp2-3).

Conclusion

Anatsui is drawn to patterns and textures, to the rich allusive power of ancient signs and to the grain of wood. With chisel, gouge, torch and chainsaw, he accelerates the processes of transformation; exploring change, decay and the impermanence of life. He constructs a clay pot, then breaks it, carves into wooden slats before gouging and burning them, rolls a disused mortar down a hill to shake off its dead parts and shape it anew. Through such seemingly destructive acts Anatsui is able to reach "a certain temperature which will make things malleable."[38] At this moment of creative intensity, metamorphosis can begin. In his hands, wood becomes cloth bearing the traces of the codes, scripts and ideograms of his African ancestors; an emblem of power and prestige. Drawing on the extensive heritage of the African continent, Anatsui reminds us of the many and varied influences which enrich us all. Whilst his works are steeped in the passing of time, El Anatsui is in no way nostalgic for some ideal or imagined past. By looking back — like the *sankofa* bird — his art points forward to regeneration and growth.

[38]Braque, Georges, *Illustrated Notebooks 1917-1955,* translated by Stanley Appelbaum. (London: Dover Publications, 1971).

Milestones

Education	1965-69	College of Art, University of Science and Technology, Kumasi, Ghana.
	1969	Postgraduate Diploma in Art Education, University of Science and Technology, Kumasi, Ghana.
Teaching Experience	1969-1975	Lecturer, Art Education Department, University of Winneba, Ghana.
	1975-1982	Lecturer, Fine and Applied Arts Department, University of Nigeria, Nsukka. (UNN)
	1982-Present	Senior Lecturer, Head of Sculpture, Fine and Applied Arts Department, UNN.
International Exchanges/ Workshops	1980	Artist-in-Residence, Cummington Community of Arts, Massachusetts, USA.
	1982-85, 1990-92	World Council Member, International Society for Education through Art (INSEA).
	1984	Zweites Symposium Nordseeküste, Cuxhaven, Germany.
	1985	Visiting Artist, Cornwall College, Redruth, UK.
	1990, 1993	International Visitors' Programme, USA.
	1996	*Images of Africa*, Helsingør and Copenhagen, Denmark.
	1996	Visiting Artist, International Peoples' College, Helsingør .
	1997	Ondambo—International Forum for African Artists, Namibia.
	1997	International Visitor, Smithsonian Institution, Washington DC, USA.
Selected Exhibitions	INDIVIDUAL	
	1976	*Wooden Wall Plaques*, Asele Art Gallery, Nsukka.
	1979	*Broken Pots: Sculpture by El Anatsui,* British Council Enugu; Institute of African Studies, University of Nigeria, Nsukka.
	1980	Wood Carvings, Community of Arts, Cummington, Massachusetts.
	1982	*Sculptures, Photographs, Drawings*, Goethe Institut, Lagos.
	1987	*Pieces of Wood: An Exhibition of Mural Sculpture,* Franco-German Auditorium, Lagos.
	1987	*Venovize: Ceramic Sculptures*, Faculty of Arts and Design, Cornwall College, Redruth.
	1991	*Old and New,* an exhibition of sculpture in assorted wood, National Museum, Lagos.
	1995	*El Anatsui*, October Gallery, London.
	1997	*Hakpa*, French Cultural Centre, Lagos.
	1998	*A Sculpted History of Africa*, October Gallery, London.

JOINT

1988	*Thoughts and Processes*, Italian Cultural Institute, Lagos (with Ndubisi Onah).
1988	*Walls and Gates*, Avant-Garde Gallery, Kaduna, Nigeria (with Liz Willis).
1996	Skoto Gallery, New York, NY (with Sol LeWitt).
1996	Contemporary African Art Gallery, New York, NY (with Tesfaye Tessema).

GROUP

1974	*Tekarts Expo 5,* Arts Centre, Accra.
1975	*Fabric Wall Hangings, Burnt Wooden Wall Plaques,* Institute of African Studies, University of Nigeria, Nsukka.
1979	*The Nsukka School,* Art Gallery of the Rivers State Council for Arts and Culture, Port Harcourt.
1979	*Christian Arts in Nigeria,* Holy Trinity Cathedral Hall, Onitsha.
1981	*Drawing on the World,* Billingham Art Gallery, Cleveland, UK; Shiples Art Gallery, Middlesborough, UK; the House of Commons, London.
1982	*Okike 10th Anniversary Exhibition,* University of Nigeria, Nsukka.
1983	*Four Contemporary African Artists,* Mintec Gallery, Port Harcourt.
1986	*Nigerian-German Prints,* University of Nigeria, Nsukka. Franco-German Auditorium, Lagos.
1986	*Aka '86—Inaugural Exhibition of the Aka Circle of Artists,* French Centre Enugu, Goethe Institut, Lagos.
1987	*Aka '87*, Hotel Presidential Enugu, National Gallery of Crafts and Design, Lagos.
1987	*Original Prints from the Third Nsukka Workshop,* University of Nigeria, Nsukka, Nigeria; Goethe Institut, Lagos.
1988	*Aka '88*, Nigerian Union of Journalists' Press Centre, Enugu; Institute of African Studies, Nsukka; National Gallery of Crafts and Design, Lagos.
1989	*Zeitgenössische Nigerianische Kunst*, Bonn, Bocholt and Mönchengladbach, Germany.
1990	*Achebe Celebration Exhibition,* Continuing Education Centre, University of Nigeria, Nsukka.
1990-1992	*Contemporary African Artists: A Changing Tradition*, a touring exhibition: Studio Museum in Harlem, New York, NY; Afro-American Historical and Cultural Museum, Philadelphia, Pennsylvania; Chicago Public Library Cultural Centre, Chicago, Illinois;.Washington Project for the Arts, Washington DC; Museum of the National Centre of African-American Artists, Boston, Massachusetts.
1990	*Five Contemporary African Artists*, 44th Venice Biennale, Venice, Italy.
1990	*Aka '90*, Presidential Hotel Enugu, Goethe Institut, Lagos.
1990	*The Calabash 1st Art Exhibition,* The Calabash, Lagos.
1991	*South of the World*, Galleria d'Arte Contemporanea, Marsala, Italy.
1991	*Sculptor's Guild of Nigeria: Inaugural Exhibition,* Murtala Mohammed Park, Enugu.
1991	*Works by a Group of African Artists,* The World Bank Art Society, Washington DC.
1991	*Aka '91*, Bona Gallery, Enugu, Goethe Institut, Lagos.
1992-1994	*Arte Amazonas*, Modern Art Museum, Rio de Janeiro, Brazil, exhibition touring as *Klima Global* to Staatliche Kunsthalle, Berlin, and Ludwig Forum, Aachen, Germany.
1992	*Aka '92*, Bona Gallery, Enugu, Didi Museum, Lagos.
1992	*Begegnung mit den Anderen*, University of Kassel, Germany.
1993	*New Currents 93: Avant-Garde Nigerian Art*, Didi Museum, Lagos.
1993	*Six African Artists*, October Gallery, London, UK.
1994	*5th Havana Biennale, Havana, Cuba.*
1994	Horniman Museum, London, UK.

1995	*Uli Art: Master Works*, Skoto Gallery, New York, NY.
1995	*Africus: 1st Johannesburg Biennale*, Johannesburg, South Africa.
1995	*Configura 2*, Erfurt, Germany.
1995-1996	*An Inside Story: African Art of Our Time*, a touring exhibition: Setagaya Art Museum, Tokyo; The Tokushima Modern Art Museum; Himeji City Museum of Arts, Himeji; Koriyama City Museum of Art, Koriyama; Marugame Inokuma-Genichiro Museum of Contemporary Art; and The Museum of Fine Arts, Gifu, Japan.
1995	*Seven Stories about Modern Art in Africa*, Whitechapel Art Gallery, London.
	The Right to Hope, touring exhibition beginning at the Johannesburg Gallery, Johannesburg, South Africa and touring to Cairo, Amman, Gaza, Jerusalem and Tel Aviv.
1995	*Contemporary Nigerian Art*, World Intellectual Property Organisation, WIPO Headquarters, Geneva, Switzerland.
1995	Osaka Triennale (Sculpture), Osaka, Japan.
1995	*Aka '95*, Bona Gallery, Enugu; Didi Museum, Lagos, Nigeria.
1996	Avant-Garde Gallery, Kaduna, Nigeria.
1996	*Transforms*, October Gallery, London.
1996	*Africana*, Sala 1, Rome, Italy.
1996	*Sju Berattelser om Modern Konst i Afrika* (Seven Stories about Modern Art in Africa), Malmö Konsthall, Malmö, Sweden.
1996	*Images of Africa*, Torpedohallen, Copenhagen.
1996	*Container 96: Art Across Oceans,* Langelinie, Copenhagen.
1996	*Transvangarde*, October Gallery, London.
1997-98	*The Poetics of Line: Seven Artists of the Nsukka Group*, National Museum of African Art, Smithsonian Institution, Washington, DC.
1998	*Riddle of the Spirits: Twelve African Artists*, Skoto Gallery, New York City, NY.
1998-99	*7th Triennial of Small Sculpture,* Stuttgart, Germany.

Prizes & Honours

Honourable Mention: First Ghana National Art Competition, 1968.
Best Student of the Year, College of Art, University of Science and Technology, Kumasi, Ghana, 1969.
Honourable Mention (joint), 44th Venice Biennale, Venice, 1990.
Kansai Telecasting Corporation Prize, Osaka Triennale (Sculpture), Japan, 1995.

Collections (Public)

African Studies Gallery, University of Nigeria, Nsukka.
Asele Institute, Nimo, Nigeria.
The Carnegie Endowment for International Peace, Washington, DC.
Diamond Bank, Victoria Island, Lagos.
Embassy of Ghana, Copenhagen.
French Cultural Centre, Lagos.
Ghana National Art Collection, Accra.
Hammermill, Hellebaek/Helsingør, Denmark.
International Peoples' College, Helsingør, Denmark.
Iwalewa-Haus, University of Bayreuth, Germany.
National Gallery of Contemporary Art, Lagos.
National Museum of African Art, Smithsonian Institution, Washington DC.
Osaka Foundation of Culture, Osaka.
Setagaya Art Museum, Tokyo.
The World Bank, Washington DC.

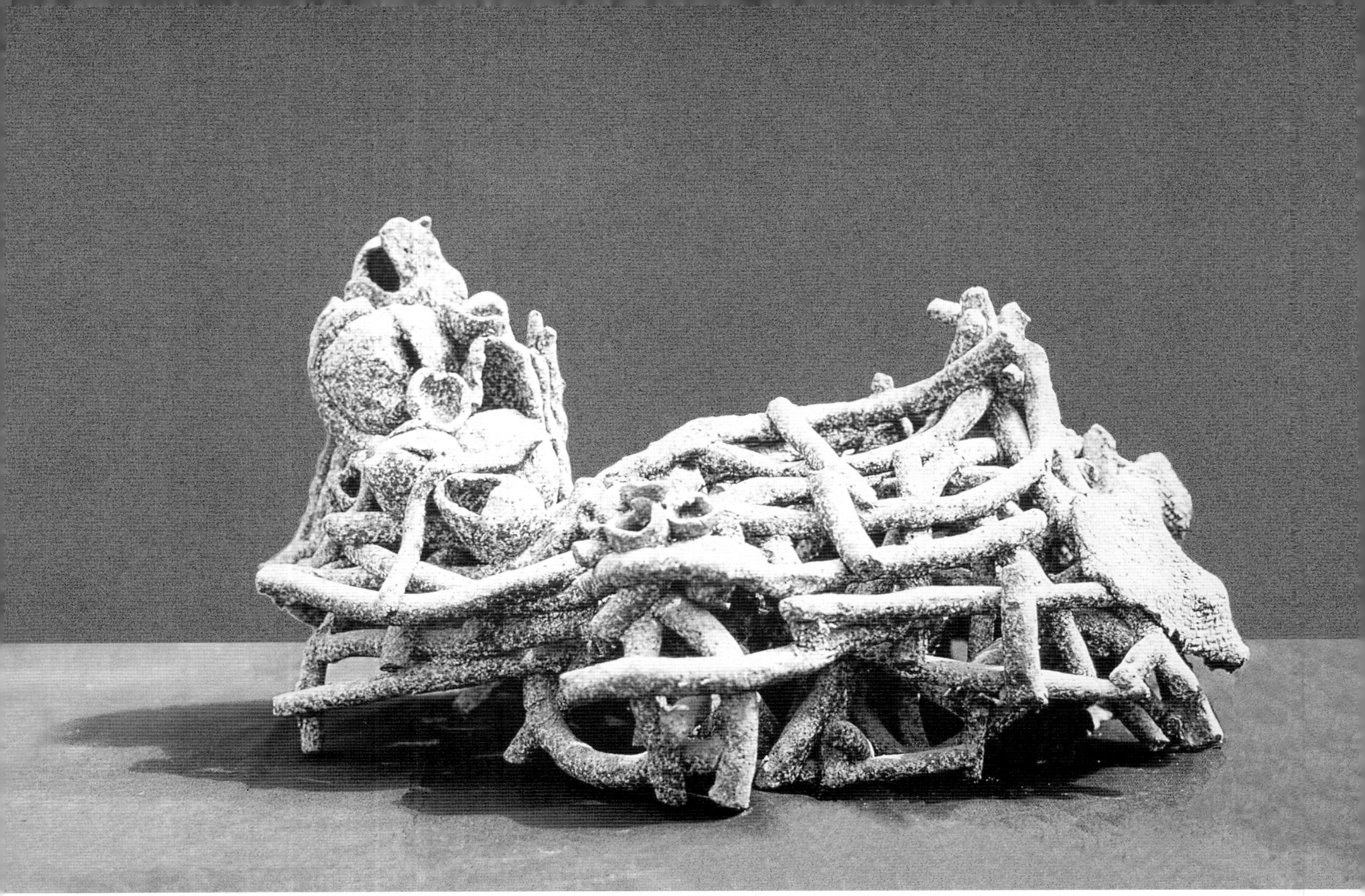

Imbroglio, 1979

ceramic-manganese body
height 50cm, width 30cm, depth 27cm

Photo: C O Amuzie

Bibliography

An Inside Story: African Art of our Time (exhibition catalogue), pp127, 188. Tokyo: Setagaya Art Museum, 1995.

Anatsui, El. Sankofa: 'Go Back an' Pick: Three Studio Notes and a Conversation,' *Third Text* (Kala Press, London), No.23, pp39-52.

Anatsui, El. *Primary Images, a book of drawings* (in progress)

Aniakor, C C, 'El Anatsui: Visual Incantations,' The International Review of African American Art. Hollywood and Los Angeles, Calif., USA, Vol 9, No 3, 1990.

Brenson, Michael, 'Contemporary Works from Africa,' *The New York Times.* New York, NY, USA, 19 January, 1990, page C32.

Cotter, Holland, 'American and Nigerian, Side by Side, El Anatsui and Sol LeWitt,' *The New York Times*, 5 July, 1996 "Art in Review."

Dwyer, G, 'A Burly North Sea Symposium: Ten Sculptors Create Works on Germany's Wet Desert,' International Sculpture, International Sculpture Centre, Washington, DC, 1985, pp8, 9.

Begegnung Mit Den Anderen (exhibition catalogue), University of Kassel, Kassel, Germany, 1992.

Configura 2: A Conversation between Obiora Udechukwu and Ulli Beier. Bayreuth: Iwalewa-Haus, University of Bayreuth, 1995.

Container 96, København Kulturby Fond '96 (exhibition catalogue). Copenhagen, Denmark, 1996, pp11, 12.

Contemporary African Artists: A Changing Tradition (exhibition catalogue). New York: Studio Museum, 1990.

Ejiogu, E. 'African Art in Transition,' African Commentary, Amherst, April 1990, pp67, 68.

Fosu, Kojo. *20th Century Art of Africa.* Zaria: Gaskiya Corporation, 1986, pp202, 205, 207, 208 and 209.

Il Sud Del Mondo (exhibition catalogue). Milan: Gabrielle Mazzotta, 1991.

Jean, 'Taet Pa Fortiden,' in *Helsingør Dagblad*, Helsingør, Denmark, 1 June, 1996, p25.

Jegede, Dele. 'Exploring the Patterns and Forms of Nature,' *The Guardian* (Lagos), 8 February 1987.

Kennedy, Jean. *New Currents, Ancient Rivers: Contemporary African Artists in a Generation of*

Change. Washington, DC: Smithsonian Institution Press, 1992, pp17, 19.
Klima Global (Arte Amazonas) (exhibition catalogue). Goethe Institut, Brasilia, Brazil, 1992.
Koplos, Janet. 'El Anatsui and Sol LeWitt at Skoto Gallery,' *Art in America*, New York, January 1997.
Leong, Leyla. 'Duas visoes sobre a Amazons,' *A Critica*, Manaus, Brazil, 14 February, 1992.
Marcoci, Roxana. *New Art*. New York: Harry N Abrams, Inc, 1997.
Nwosu, Chinye. 'Anatsui's Pieces of Wood,' *Lagos Life*, Lagos, 26 February-4 March, 1987, p11.
Oguibe, Olu. 'Africa Storms the Venice Biennale,' *Home News* (London), 7-13 June, 1990, p21.
Oguibe, Olu. 'El Anatsui in the Public Space,' *Third Text*, (Kala Press, London), No. 23, pp69-77.
Okeke, Chika. 'The Quest: from Zaria to Nsukka,' *Seven Stories about Modern Art in Africa*, Whitechapel Art Gallery, London, pp58-59.
Okeke, Chika. 'Slashing Wood, Eroding Culture: Conversation with El Anatsui,' *NKA*, Journal of Contemporary African Art, 1994, Issue 1.
Oguibe, O, 'Beyond Death and Nothingness,' *African Arts*, UCLA, Vol XXXI, No 1, 1998, pp48-55.
Oloidi, Ola, 'Who Are the New African Artists?' *Aspects of African Spirit,* Chrysalis. (Swedenborg Foundation, New York, USA), Vol III, Issue 1.
Ottenberg, Simon. 'El Anatsui: Colourful Woods and Dark Lines,' *New Traditions from Nigeria: Seven Artists of the Nsukka Group.*Washington, DC: Smithsonian Institution Press, 1997, chapter 9, pp154-179.
Péri-Willis, E A, El Anatsui at the October Gallery, London, *NKA*, Journal of Contemporary African Art, 1996, Issue 4, p70-71.
Plagens, Peter. 'Africa Meets the West: Three New Exhibitions Capture the Spirit and Struggle of Black Artists on Two Continents,' *Newsweek,* NewYork, 19 January, 1990.
Ro, Eun Nim. 'On the North Sea Symposium,' *Space, Environment, Architecture and Art* (Seoul), 1995, Vol 1, pp15-157.
The Right To Hope (exhibition catalogue). London: Earthscan Publications, 1995.
Wallach, Amei. 'The New African Tradition,' *Newsday*, New York, NY, 28 January, 1990, pp16-17.
Wokoun, Alois. 'Hradby a Brany Sochare Anatsuiho,' *Novy Orient,* 10/89, Prague, Rocnit 44, 1989, pp302 -305.
XLIV Expositione Internazionale d'Arte: La Biennale di Venezia (exhibition catalogue). Fabbri Editori, 1990.
Zweites Symposium Nordseeküste: Künstler vor dem Deich (exhibition catalogue), Cuxhaven, Germany, 1984.

Films and Video

Zweites Symposium Nordseeküste, Cuxhaven, Germany, 1984.
Kindred Spirits: Contemporary Nigerian Artists, Smithsonian World, USA, 1990.
XLIV Expositione Internationale d'Arte, La Biennale di Venezia, Studio Mestiere Cinema, Italy, 1990.
Arte Amazonas, John Arden, Brazil, 1992.
West Africa: Art and Identities, Nick Levinson and Catherine King, BBC Open University, London, 1998.
Ondambo, Arandis, Namibia, 1998.

Index

adinkra, 19, 35, 67, 80, 81, 85, 86, 88
Adinsibuli Stood Tall, 34, 35, 36, 37
Africa - Internal Rhythms II, 41
Akua's Surviving Children, 26, 38, 39, 64, 67, 68, 84, 87, 88
Akuaba, 80, 87
Ampofo, Oku, 79
Ancestors Converged Again, The, 46, 47, 87
Ancient Cloth Series VIII, 53
Aniakor, Chike, 73, 93
An Inside Story: African Art of Our Time, 61, 69
Antubam, Kofi, 79
Arte Amazonas, 83, 85, 86
Asante *adinkra* cloth, 19
Asante (ashante, ashanti), 24, 31, 33, 36, 67, 80, 85
At the Ancestors Conference, 49, 77, 82

Broken Pots, 69, 84

Chambers of Memory, 22, 78, 79, 84

Douglas-Camp, Sokari, 21

Earth-Moon Connection, 42, 88
Erosion, 30, 51, 70, 83, 85
Ewe, 24, 25, 29, 31, 33, 59, 67, 79, 80, 81, 83, 85, 87, 88
Fosu, Kojo, 17, 79

Glover, Ablade, 31, 59

Igbo, 18, 24, 25, 32, 35, 67, 74, 81, 82
Images of Africa, 83, 87
Imbroglio, 92

Kenté cloth, 81
Kindred Spirits, 65
Kumasi, 19, 24, 31, 59, 68,79, 80

Leopard Cloth, 55, 85, 86
Leopard Secret Society (ekpé), 19, 33, 82, 86
Lewitt, Sol, 65, 86

Mammoth Crowd Series I, 48
Moon and Stars, 52

National Museum of African Art, Washington DC, 25, 83
Natural Synthesis, 18, 25, 32, 34, 68, 81
Nok Sculpture, 33, 69, 74, 82, 83, 84
nsibidi, 19, 33, 35, 67, 82, 85, 88
Nsukka Group, 36, 59, 69, 82, 83, 87

October Gallery, 28, 29, 31, 83
Offering to the Weather, 96
Okeke, Chika, 34, 67, 94
Okeke, Uche, 18, 19, 22, 32, 33, 34, 68, 81, 82
Old and New, 85, 86
On their Fateful Journey Nowhere, 2, 3, 35, 36, 61, 81, 87, 88
Onabolu, Aina, 18
Onobrakpeya, Bruce, 18, 19, 22
Ottenberg, Simon, 84, 94

Patches of History III, 43, 82
Picasso, Pablo, 32, 73, 76

Remnant of Grandma's Cloth, 45, 85, 88

sankofa and sankofa bird, 31, 32, 34, 72, 74, 80, 81, 88
Skoto Gallery, New York, 86, 91
slave trade, 23, 67, 68, 87
Studio Museum Harlem: *A Changing Tradition,* 18, 57, 83, 93

Tapper, 34, 50, 87, 88
Transvangarde, 27, 29, 31, 34, 36, 66

uli, 18, 19, 32, 33, 35, 67, 81, 84, 88
Undercurrents, 44
Unfolding the Scroll of History II, 10, 15, 40

Venice Biennale, 17, 18, 19, 21, 25, 61, 83, 94
Visa Queue, 12, 15, 88

When I last wrote to you about Africa, 73
Whitechapel Art Gallery, 83
Wonder Masquerade II, 54, 85

Zaria Art Society, 32, 68, 81

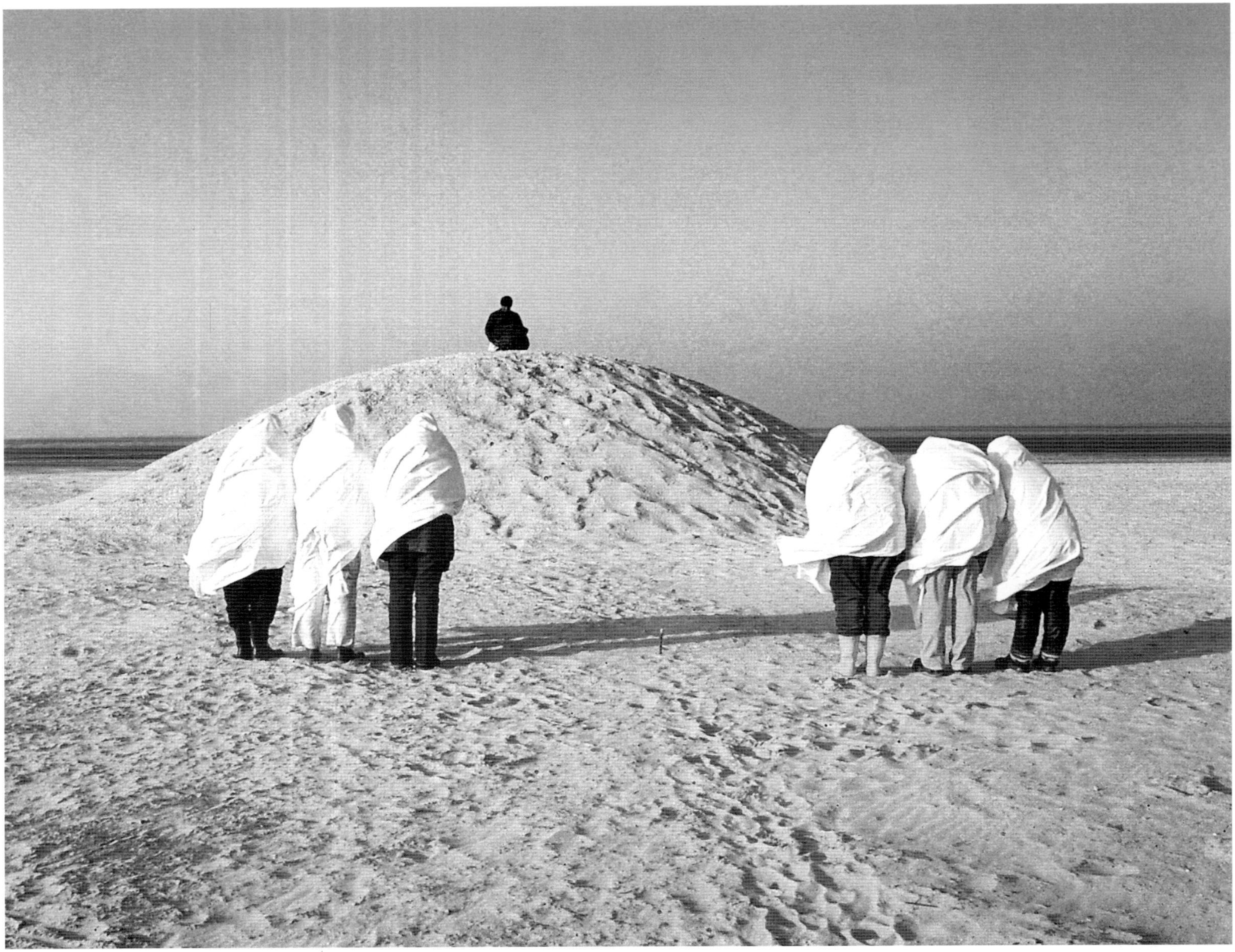

Offering to the Weather, 1984
(Zweites Symposium Nordseeküste, Cuxhaven, Germany)

installation and performance, sand & ceramic pots, height circa 3m, diametre circa 8m

Photo: Ottmar von Poschinger